The Story of JOSEPH

HOW GOD
CAN REDEEM
IMPERFECT FAMILIES

ERIN DAVIS

MOODY PUBLISHERS
CHICAGO

All emphasis in Scripture has been added.

Published in association with Wolgemuth and Wilson.

Edited by Amanda Cleary Eastep
Cover and interior design: Brittany Schrock
Cover graphic of watercolor stain copyright © 2024 by Alex/Adobe Stock (295439226). All rights reserved.
Cover graphic of branches copyright © 2024 by Iyubox1148/Adobe Stock (134815408). All rights reserved.
Interior illustration of family tree © 2017 by Pro/iStock (638473512). All rights reserved.
Interior illustration of mandrake © 2021 by Anitapol/Shutterstock (2004595694). All rights reserved.

ISBN: 978-0-8024-3456-2

Originally delivered by fleets of horse-drawn wagons, the affordable paperbacks from D. L. Moody's publishing house resourced the church and served everyday people. Now, after more than 125 years of publishing and ministry, Moody Publishers' mission remains the same—even if our delivery systems have changed a bit. For more information on other books (and resources) created from a biblical perspective, go to www.moodypublishers.com or write to:

Moody Publishers
820 N. LaSalle Boulevard
Chicago, IL 60610

1 3 5 7 9 10 8 6 4 2

Printed in the United States of America

To my great, great, great granddaughters.
I cannot wait to meet you in heaven.

CONTENTS

Week 5: Blessings & Curses

Week 6: Reunions, Reconciliation & Redemption

Week 7: I Am a String in the Bow of the Lord

Week 8: Nurseries for Heaven

STUDY INTRODUCTION

This is not a study about Joseph. It's not ultimately about family either.

This is a study about God.

The story of Joseph matters. So much so, that the Holy Spirit has preserved it for millennia. The tales of brotherly betrayal, a technicolor dream coat, and jailhouse redemption have been told and retold in countless Sunday school classrooms, vacation Bible schools, and living room circles. Still, the point of Scripture is not merely to tell good stories, **but to reveal the heart of a good God.**

That significant but often subtle shift will inform how we move through the story of Joseph. As we dig into this amazing and ancient story, we will often pause to ask: What does this reveal about God? Because when we rightly see God, we can rightly see everything else—including our imperfect families.

Without God, Joseph's story could be nothing more than a series of mistakes and misunderstandings. *Because of God*, it is a tale for the ages, one that will surely give you fresh perspective and passion for the people on your family tree.

You Never Study Alone

Bible study can be hard work. Your brain will need to clear cultural hurdles to see Joseph's story as the writer intended. There are names and places to keep track of and constant distractions tugging at your attention span. You cannot do this alone. Good news! You don't have to. Consider Jesus' words from John 16:

> When the Spirit of truth comes, **he will guide you into all the truth**, for he will not speak on his own authority, but whatever he hears he will speak, and he will declare to you the things that are to come. **He will glorify me**, for he will take what is mine and declare it to you. (vv. 13–14)

If you are a follower of Jesus, the Holy Spirit is with you. In fact, dear Christian, He is *within you*! He will guide you to what is true and help you see the glory and goodness of God on every page of your Bible.

- When you are stuck, ask the Spirit for help.
- When your motivation to study Scripture is weak, ask the Spirit for help.
- When God's Word convicts or calls you to obedience, ask the Spirit for help.

It All Matters

One North Star for my approach to Scripture has long been 2 Timothy 3:16–17, which states, "All Scripture is breathed out by God and profitable for teaching, for reproof, for correction, and for training in righteousness, that the man of God may be complete, equipped for every good work."

Mind if I give the Erin Davis translation? *All* Scripture is inspired, so it *all* matters and God uses it *all* to make us more like Him.

We won't skip the challenging passages in Joseph's story or pretend there aren't parts of it that make us uncomfortable, alarmed, or agitated. This is part of developing the discipline of *putting ourselves under the authority of the whole Bible.*

What and So What

You'll find a **"What"** statement printed in bold at the beginning of each week's session. This phrase is meant to prompt you to ask, "What am I looking for?" These themes work together to build a foundational understanding of God's good design for your family. You'll also find the **"So What?"** This is meant to move you from observation and interpretation of Scripture to application, because the Bible is not just a book of theories. It has the power to transform the way you live your actual life.

As you open the Scriptures again and again, day after day, you can be confident that God will use His Word to challenge and change you. *It's what He does!*

Some of you are wired like me, Type A all the way, which probably means you like to know the game plan before you get started. Sister, I got you.

Each week's session contains four days of traditional homework. For busy women like you and me, that pace might feel overwhelming, but I'm a big believer that *whoever is doing the work is doing the learning.* There is simply no substitute for rolling up your sleeves and digging into the Bible yourself.

The fifth day changes the pattern. Rather than Bible study, this day is set aside for intentional prayer for your family. These are not meant to be throwaway lessons. In fact, I am asking God to do something generationally significant through your prayers.

Can I give you some advice from someone who's been there? Don't try to cram your whole week of sessions into the thirty minutes before your Bible study meets. **The goal of meaningful study is not to tick a box but to enjoy the precious and powerful Word of God**. Ask the Lord to guide you to the perfect tension of being stretched so you'll grow, but at a pace that is sustainable. It will require effort and stick-to-itiveness, but it will be worth every sacrifice.

May I make one more suggestion before we dig in? Find some other women to do this study with you. My heart and mind have been radically changed by this practice. The Bible is true no matter what, but there is a compounding that happens when we dig into it together. Since everyone has a family, and everyone's family needs hope, I am confident you can find a friend or two (or a larger group) to go through this study with you.

We have a motto among the group of women who gather in my home each week: "No Bible study dropouts." If you get behind, set aside some time to catch up. *Just don't quit.* Let's finish this together, deal? If you're studying with a group, you can find a free Leaders Guide on my website ErinDavis.org.

As you open your Bible day after day, you'll gain more than help and hope for your family—you'll get a bigger picture of God. Is there any endeavor more worthwhile?

Before you dig in, take time to pray. Ask the Lord to help you see Him in Joseph's story and then to reorient your life to His will and ways. Write out your prayer below.

From Generation to Generation

what:

Family is God's idea.

so what?

Intentionally consider what kind of family you want to build.

WEEK 1

Beginning in the first chapter of the first book of the Bible, it's evident that family is God's good plan for the flourishing of mankind. And it doesn't take long for Satan to slither in seeking to destroy it. In this session, you'll lay a foundation by building a biblical definition of family.

It's time for me to say my favorite words . . . **open your Bible** to Genesis 50. As we dig into the story of Joseph, let's start at the end.

WEEK 1 | DAY 1

BEGINNING AT THE END

Big idea: *Building a God-honoring family requires intention.*

READ GENESIS 50:22–26

Start with what you know. When you think of the story of Joseph, what comes to mind? Make a list below.

(If you're new to the Bible or to Joseph's story, hooray! I'm so glad you're here. It's okay to leave this space blank. You're going to have a lot to fill in soon.)

Revisit Genesis 50:22–26. What details of Joseph's life can you add?

Long after the day of Joseph's funeral, another patriarch had something interesting to say about the value of such sad occasions. King Solomon was the wisest man to ever live (1 Kings 3:12). God gifted him with a unique ability to see life and death through a truth-shaped lens. Solomon wrote:

> It is better to go to the house of mourning
> than to go to the house of feasting,
> for this is the end of all mankind,
> and the living will lay it to heart.
> ECCLESIASTES 7:2

What point do you think Solomon was trying to make?

We can paraphrase that passage with this dichotomy: funerals and festivals. If we have to pick one of the two, wise Solomon says, "Pick the funeral."

That's not exactly a happy thought, but unless the Lord returns first, there will come a day when you and I are the ones in the coffin and the families we are building today will be gathered around *our* bodies.

It's a sobering reality. Here's one equally sobering: When your life is over, what will your family say about you? Were you a source of joy, comfort, and wisdom to them? Or, were you critical, easily angered, and constantly offended? What will they say you built your family life around? Was it love, charity, faith, or fun (one of my favorites!)? Or something else?

Based on the description of Joseph's funeral, what can you discern about his legacy?

We know Joseph lived a long life: one hundred and ten years filled with high highs and low lows, providentially stitched together by the presence and power of God. He died surrounded by his brothers and children. Though there are many things worth saying in such moments, Joseph wanted to talk about his promise-keeping God.

Look at verses 24 and 25 again. What do you think Joseph was trying to express?

Perhaps it seems strange to start a study of Joseph's life with his funeral, but events like this have a way of distilling things down to what is absolutely true. In this snapshot of the end of Joseph's life, we see what lasts: faith and family. We also see that God-honoring families don't just happen. They are built, one decision at a time.

GOD-HONORING FAMILIES
DON'T JUST HAPPEN.
THEY ARE BUILT,
ONE DECISION AT A TIME.

Joseph's legacy wasn't buried in Egypt. We're still thinking about it today. And by God's good plan, your story won't end with you. As we will see in the days ahead, part of His vision for our families is that they are a means by which His blessings are passed from generation to generation. We have the privilege of cooperating with Him in what He wants to do through our families.

Think about the end of your life. Who do you hope is gathered around you on that day? I doubt you're picturing the faces of your coworkers or social media followers. More likely it's the man you vowed to love "until death do us part," the children or grandchildren you adore, or the extended family you've spent countless holiday dinners beside. This mental exercise reminds us that family matters. Still, building God-honoring families requires constant Spirit-enabled, flesh-denying, countercultural work.

Write out Psalm 127:1 below.

I'm fond of the New Living Translation version of this verse:

> Unless the LORD builds a house,
> the work of the builders is wasted.
> Unless the LORD protects a city,
> guarding it with sentries will do no good. (NLT)

The point of Bible study is never to try harder and do better in our own strength. (I'm sure you've already noticed that no amount of human effort can result in perfect families.) But Joseph's story dramatically illustrates that God can make beauty out of brokenness. He alone can take our families and turn them into something that lasts forever.

As you wrap up today's study, take the time to think carefully and critically about what you want God to do through your family, using the prompts below.

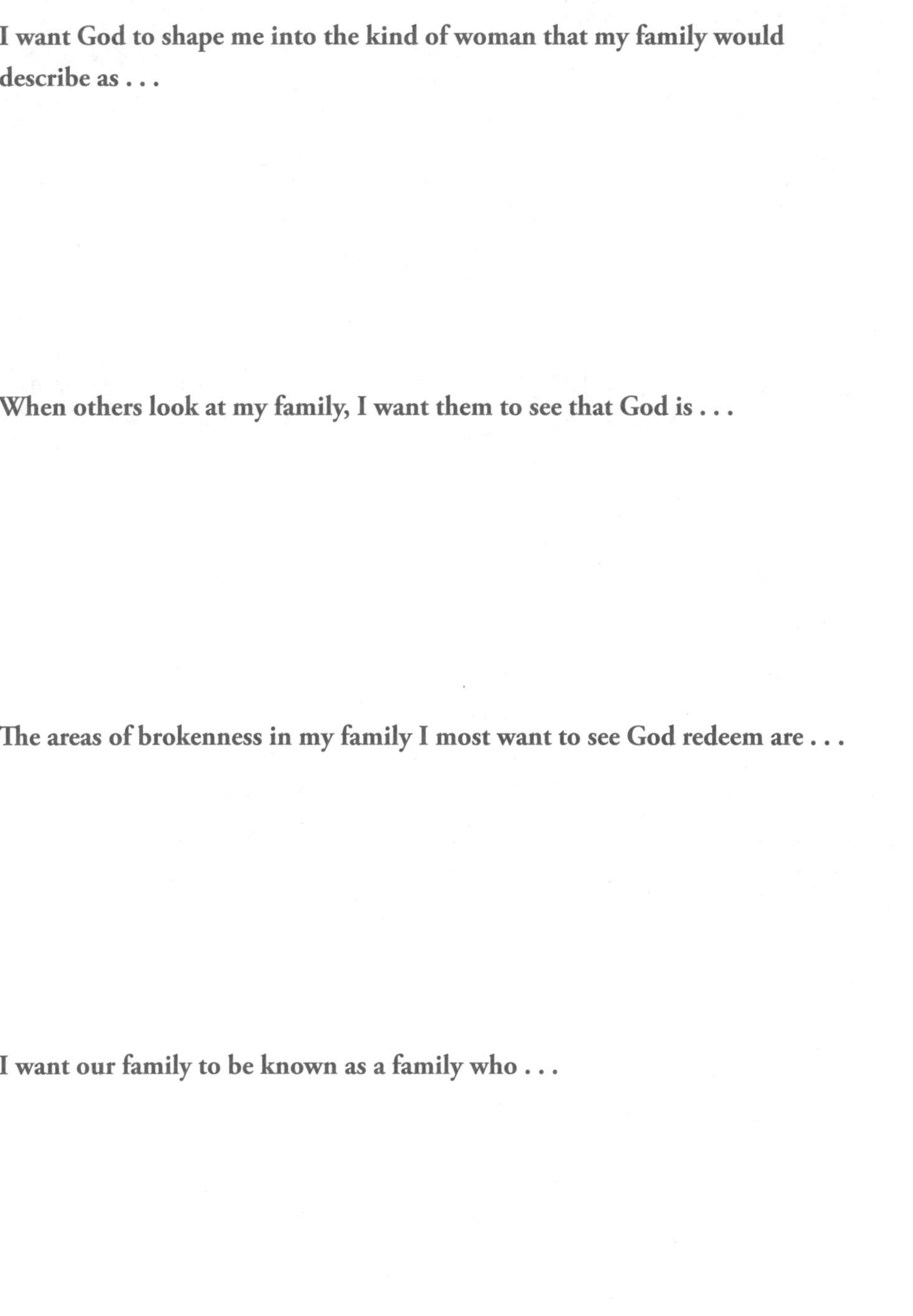

I want God to shape me into the kind of woman that my family would describe as . . .

When others look at my family, I want them to see that God is . . .

The areas of brokenness in my family I most want to see God redeem are . . .

I want our family to be known as a family who . . .

WEEK 1 | DAY 2

A PLAN FOR FLOURISHING

Big Idea: *Family is God's idea*

READ GENESIS 1:26–31, 2:18–25

Some of my earliest and fondest memories involve playing "family" as a little girl. I made a bridal veil out of a white pillowcase, pulled some wildflowers from the front yard for a bouquet, and forced my little brother to pretend to be the groom. Or I'd rock and sing to my baby dolls and tell them, "I'm your mommy." Unlike the alphabet or counting to a hundred, no one had to teach me the value of family.

Write down some of your earliest family memories.

Consider the grand narrative of Scripture. Family is a prominent theme. Noah escaped the flood of God's judgment with his family (Gen. 6–7). The Israelites fled

Egypt with their families (Ex. 12:31–38). Jesus Himself was born into a family. *He chose* to experience firsthand the discipline of a parent (Luke 2:41–52), the pestering of a sibling (Mark 3:20–35), and the expectations of aunts, uncles, and cousins (Luke 1:39–45).

When you think about families in the Bible, what other stories come to mind? Make a list.

Review Genesis 1:26–31. What observations can you make about God's design for the first human family?

Humans aren't the only ones with families, you know? The Madagascar tenrec deserves a lot of flowers on Mother's Day. She is the mammal with the largest litters, often birthing 30+ babies at once.[1] Wolves, beavers, and vultures are among the many creatures that mate for life.[2] **But humans are distinct in that we bear the image of God. This has implications for the way we see the purpose of our families.** When God made the first family, and every family since, He made something special—something *set apart.*

Though the world began with God's creation of light and dark, land and sea, and creatures of all shapes and sizes, the text reveals that the first human family was not an afterthought, but an essential part of God's plan for the world He made.

Where Genesis 1 records the creation of the first image bearers of God, Genesis 2 captures the very first wedding.

Write out Genesis 2:24–25 below.

Look at that passage again. Circle any words or phrases that intrigue you.

Did you circle "hold fast," "one flesh," or "not ashamed"? Scripture gives us a vision of the perfect shalom God intends for our families. The sinless intimacy enjoyed by the first couple feels like a dream to those of us who have been marred by the fall. But my, how our hearts do long for it.

Connect the dots between Genesis 1 and 2 to see that God's good design for families goes well beyond giving Adam and Eve a happy home.

Revisit Genesis 1:28.

Write a synonym for each of the words God used in His instructions to the first family.

Fruitful ____________ Multiply ____________

Fill ____________ Subdue ____________

Have dominion ____________

Write the assignment God gave to Adam and Eve in your own words.

God's intent for the first family was that they would play a vital role in ruling the world He made. **His design hasn't changed.** Families remain a fundamental building block for human flourishing. The reverse is also true: When the family crumbles, the implications for God's world are catastrophic.

God's heart for families is not limited to the first two chapters of the Bible.

Thinking big picture about the Bible, answer the following questions:

How are families addressed in the Ten Commandments? (Check out Exodus 20:12–15).

What role did families play in God's covenants to Abraham, Moses, and David?

Do the Psalms and Proverbs address families?

How does God use family language to express His relationship with His people?

Bottom line: Family is God's idea. Circle back to Genesis 1 one more time. **Review verse 31.**

When God observed all of creation, crowned with the first family, how did He describe it?

Based on what you've read in this session, how do you define family? Write your definition below.

Throughout the rest of this study (and beyond), I'd encourage you to define family this way:

Family: an institution designed by God to reveal who He is and to subdue and cultivate the world He has made.

How is this different from the definition of family often offered by the world?

How does a biblically based definition of family change the way you see the purpose of your family?

Though God's design is perfect, none of us have picture-perfect families. In Day 4 of this Week, you'll see that Adam and Eve's family was fractured soon after it began. Throughout this study, you'll find that Joseph's family could have made a heated episode of a popular reality show. But what is true about the first family is true of Joseph's family and is true of yours and mine: **God is working to redeem even the most broken families.** You can participate in His redemptive work by expressing your desire for God to use your family to accomplish His good plan.

Wrap up today's study by writing out a prayer, asking God to fulfill His vision through your family.

WEEK 1 | DAY 3

DON'T SKIP THE BEGATS

Big Idea: *God is doing a generational work through your family.*

READ PSALM 145

When each of my sons made the decision to get baptized, I reached out to their grandparents, aunts, uncles, and cousins and asked them to write a letter sharing a bit about their own walk with Jesus. My children are still too young to fully appreciate their family legacy of faith, but I've often flipped through their binders of letters and marveled at God's faithfulness. Though each person must make the personal decision to bow the knee to Jesus, when I look at the big picture, it's clear that He has been at work in my family for generations. He's doing a generational work in your family too.

Think about your extended family: parents, grandparents, siblings, aunts, and uncles. **As you think about their lives, what evidence do you see of God at work? Write down what comes to mind. Be specific.**

In the ancient Middle Eastern culture where Joseph's story is set, family was everything. In our modern, Western world we tend to see family ties more loosely. This can cause us to miss or misunderstand the emphasis on family lines that's so prominent in the Bible.

Read through the genealogies from Genesis 5 and Matthew 1 referenced below. Resist the temptation to skim or skip. In the space below each, record any repeated words or phrases as you read.

Genesis 5:1–32	Matthew 1:1–17

These are two of the hundreds of genealogies recorded in Scripture.

Circling back to the guiding principle of 2 Timothy 3:16–17 that all Scripture is God-breathed and useful for shaping us into the image of God, why do you think God inspired the Bible writers to record so many family lists?

Remember that though the Bible contains many stories of people, it is ultimately a book about God. **Does that change your answer above? What do genealogies reveal about God?**

Look up the following verses. Next to each reference write down what it reveals about God's heart for families.

Exodus 3:15

Psalm 78:1–7

Psalm 90:1–2

Daniel 4:3

Scripture contains many generational commands, blessings, and curses, demonstrating that He is always doing more than what happens in your lifetime. Here are two principles to keep in mind:

1. God is at work in every generation.
2. God is at work across *all* generations.

Your view is limited. You might know some things about what He is doing in two or three generations of your family today. Only God sees human history from beginning to end. Only He knows how the ways He works today will impact your family one thousand years from now.

Read through Psalm 145 again. This time circle the word "all" each time you come to it.

In my Bible I've labeled this "The All Psalm." It's all about the goodness and greatness of God. **Circle back to verses 4–7. What does this passage add to your understanding of God's design for families?**

The passing of the baton of faith from one generation to another is one way families can contribute to human flourishing.

How have the previous generations of your family impacted your faith? Be specific.

Though Joseph will be our focus for much of this study, he's really just one pixel in the bigger picture of what God is doing. His Word encourages us to zoom out and dare to ask, "What is God doing beyond the scope of what I see and know?" *and* "How can I partner with God to build a legacy of faith in my family?"

Meditating on the goodness and greatness of God through His Word is a worthy exercise, but it shouldn't stop with you.

How can you commend the works of God to the generations before and after you today? Make a list and then ask the Lord to direct you and help you prioritize.

WEEK 1 | DAY 4

OPPOSED!

Big idea: *The enemy hates your family.*

READ GENESIS 3

Our oldest son was barely the size of a lime the first time we became aware of the devil's intent to destroy him. I was four months pregnant when a routine ultrasound exposed a catastrophic problem with his development. We were referred to a specialist who looked at his image on the screen and then looked at us and said, "Your baby will not survive the pregnancy. If he does, he will be severely handicapped. I suggest you abort him."

As I write these words, that tiny baby is sixteen years old. He is healthy and handsome. His name is Elisha, which means "my God saves." He is starting to develop his own faith in and commitment to Jesus. He has a growing passion for his lost friends at school. He's beginning to imagine how He can serve the Lord in the years ahead.

There's a famous line in the story of Joseph. We'll spend more time on it later in the study, but it's also fitting here. Genesis 50:20 states: "As for you, you meant evil against me, but God meant it for good, to bring it about that many people should be kept alive, as they are today."

In hindsight, it's clear to me for various reasons that the enemy's intent was to snuff out my son's life before he had the chance to breathe his first breath. If you and I could have a long chat over a steaming cup of tea, I'm confident we'd see evidence that he has fired his flaming darts at your family too.

Revisit Genesis 3. Does thinking about Adam and Eve as the first family change the way you see this interaction? Write down your thoughts.

Zero in on verses 8–13. What effect did sin have on Adam and Eve's relationship with each other?

On their relationship with God?

Consider the curse handed down by God in verses 14–19. How would sin impact Adam and Eve's family life moving forward? Be specific.

Do you see evidence of the curse in your own family life? Explain.

The perfect shalom peace and intimacy for which God created the first family was shattered by Adam and Eve's rebellion. Every family since has struggled under the weight of sin's devastating consequences. It's not just your family. It's not just mine. Sin has sent shockwaves through every generation east of Eden.

Read John 10:10. According to this verse, what is Satan's mission?

Based on what you learned from Genesis 1:27, why do you think Satan attacks God's people so relentlessly?

What began in the garden has continued throughout human history. One example is the attacks on children recorded in the Bible. The author of Joseph's story, Moses, could have been killed by one such aggression.

Read Exodus 1:8–22.

What did Pharaoh command to be done to all Hebrew male babies? (vv. 16, 22)

As a mother of four sons, I can barely stomach the brutality of this story. I don't want to think about giving birth to my babies in a world where a jealous ruler could order them murdered and thrown into a river, yet that's exactly what Scripture records. It would be bad enough if such evil was contained to a single moment in history. *It wasn't.*

Read Matthew 2:13–18. These verses describe a different era and an entirely different spot on the globe. But this time, Moses wasn't the baby boy who God supernaturally protected. It was Jesus.

Revisit verse 13. What was Herod's intent?

Sound familiar? Remind yourself, what is Satan's mission? (John 10:10)

When Herod's attempt to kill Jesus was thwarted, how did he respond? (v. 16)

Think generationally. What did Satan stand to gain by wiping out all of the baby boys?

Think about our world today. Do you see any evidence that Satan is still seeking to destroy children and families? Write down your observations.

Take a quick jump with me to Ephesians 5:31–33. Here you will find the verses we read in Genesis 2 repeated with an application that goes far beyond Adam and Eve's union. **Based on these verses, how do you define the purpose of Christian marriage?**

If marriage is meant to display the mystery and beauty of Jesus' love for the church, and children are meant to be a means to fulfill God's command to be fruitful and multiply (Gen. 1:28), no wonder Satan opposes our families!

Mind if I repeat myself?

IF MARRIAGE IS MEANT TO DISPLAY THE MYSTERY AND BEAUTY OF JESUS' LOVE FOR THE CHURCH, AND CHILDREN ARE MEANT TO BE A MEANS TO FULFILL GOD'S COMMAND TO BE FRUITFUL AND MULTIPLY, NO WONDER SATAN OPPOSES OUR FAMILIES!

There is more at stake here than the happiness of those who share your last name. **Your family is meant to be a picture of God's love and a means to fulfill His mission in the world.** Because of this, your family is opposed by the enemy of God, who seeks to sabotage all that God has created.

Widen the lens from what you just read in Ephesians 5:31–33 and you will see that *it was in the context of describing family life* that Paul wrote, "For we do not wrestle against flesh and blood, but against the rulers, against the authorities, against the cosmic powers over this present darkness, against the spiritual forces of evil in the heavenly places" (Eph. 6:12).

How does the perspective that Satan opposes your family shift the way you see your current victories and challenges?

- Does it seem like Christian marriage is constantly under attack? **It is!**
- Are there dark forces behind the cultural messages trying to pull your children away from the truth? **There are!**
- Does it feel like something or someone is always trying to tear your family apart? **There is.**
- Does building a God-honoring family on the bedrock truth of God's Word feel like a radical act of rebellion in our day? **It is!**

One of the blessings of digging into God's Word is that it helps us see beyond our limited perspective. The battle between light and darkness is bigger than each of us, but so is God's work to redeem it. As we study Joseph's story, we will see these two forces constantly at play, but the victor is never in question. In many ways, Joseph's life beautifully illustrates the truth recorded in 1 John 4:4: "For he who is in you is greater than he who is in the world." Amen?

Facing the reality of Satan's opposition to our families is not meant to cause us to cower in fear. Instead, it can wake us up to what's really on the line and inspire us to fight for our families as a means of pushing back the darkness.

As you wrap up today's study, meditate on Psalm 127 (you wrote out verse 1 of this psalm on Day 1). This passage is filled with family language, but it's also a warrior psalm. Read and reread it, asking the Spirit to show you how He wants to use your family in the battle against evil.

> Unless the Lord builds the house,
> those who build it labor in vain.
> Unless the Lord watches over the city,
> the watchman stays awake in vain.
>
> It is in vain that you rise up early
> and go late to rest,
> eating the bread of anxious toil;
> for he gives to his beloved sleep.
>
> Behold, children are a heritage from the Lord,
> the fruit of the womb a reward.
> Like arrows in the hand of a warrior
> are the children of one's youth.
>
> Blessed is the man
> who fills his quiver with them!
> He shall not be put to shame
> when he speaks with his enemies in the gate.

WEEK 1 | DAY 5

LEAVE A LEGACY OF PRAYER

You can have a profound influence on your family by developing the discipline of prayer. **Take time today to intercede for your family. Use the prompts below as a guide.**

Write down the names of the family members you want to pray for today. Next to each name, write down one need you want to see God meet.

Are there patterns of sin and brokenness that you need God to interrupt? Make a list and pray through it.

What about your family can you praise God for today?

What generational work do you want to see God do in your family? Write it out as a prayer.

Write out Numbers 6:24–26 as a prayer of blessing for your family.

A Crooked Family Tree

what:

Every family has its share of crooked branches, gnarled by sin, disappointment, mistakes, betrayals, trauma, rebellion, and grief.

so what?

There is room for God to work in every family, even yours.

"Father Abraham had many sons.
Many sons had Father Abraham.
And they were liars; and cheaters too.
And sometimes they stole women and children.
Right arm. Left arm."[3]

Perhaps there's a reason why some of our children's music tends to be a little vague on the details. Certainly, the specifics of Joseph's family are enough to keep your average Sunday school teacher up at night praying that that one extra curious learner is graciously absent from class this week.

WEEK 2

As we dive deeper into Joseph's family tree this week, we'll find swindlers and sinners, feuds and fractures, bad blood and sibling squabbles. Most of it doesn't get wrapped up in tidy bows, either. When we study the Scriptures systematically, we are forced to face the tension that God works in the midst of the mess more often than He works in the absence of it.

WHEN WE STUDY THE SCRIPTURES SYSTEMATICALLY, WE ARE FORCED TO FACE THE TENSION THAT GOD WORKS IN THE MIDST OF THE MESS MORE OFTEN THAN HE WORKS IN THE ABSENCE OF IT.

This provides practical comfort because your family is messy too. (So is mine.) But when you read this week's passages, resist making them all about you. The Bible is first and foremost a book about God. *His* character is what gives us true hope for the challenges our families face.

It's time for me to say those favorite words again . . . **open your Bible** to Genesis 12. Joseph's family tree was planted with the seed of an audacious promise.

WEEK 2 | DAY 1

A HERITAGE OF PROMISE

Big Idea: *Perfection is not a prerequisite for God's goodness.*

READ GENESIS 12:2–3

Aren't you glad the fall was not fatal for mankind? It's true that Adam and Eve's sin forever fractured their family, and yours, but that's not the end of the story. As the book of Genesis unfolds, we still see God building and blessing families. Adam and Eve fulfilled their commission to fill the earth and subdue it. Genesis 5 draws the branches of a rapidly expanding family tree. Eventually, Adam's great, great, great, great, great, great grandson Noah was born in an age where wickedness was so rampant that "the LORD regretted that he had made man on the earth, and it grieved him to his heart" (Gen. 6:6).

You know the story. The Lord sent a flood of judgment to wipe out His image bearers, but He chose to preserve not one man, not even one couple, but one *family*. Noah and his sons and daughters-in-law were spared from God's wrath on the ark God commanded them to build (Gen. 7:1).

Look up Genesis 8:19. According to this verse, how did the animals exit the ark?

It all sounds so warm and fuzzy (if you refuse to think about everyone else drowning), except the part where Noah got drunk and cursed his youngest son (Gen. 9:20–25). Even the great heroes of our faith, like Noah, sinned, hurt others, and raised imperfect kids. **There is not a single chapter in the Bible about perfect people, but there's page after page about the redemption of God**.

Genesis 12 brings us to an important juncture in the beginnings of Joseph's story. From memory, do you know what relationship Abraham had to Joseph (e.g., father, grandfather)?

It's okay if you don't know. We'll build Joseph's family tree together in this session. For now, let's focus on a special promise God made Abraham.

Revisit Genesis 12:1–3. Write down the specific commitments God made to Abraham.

The Lord appeared to Abraham again in **Genesis 18:17–19. Read those verses and record the specific commitments God made to Abraham.**

Remember, that we've defined family this way:

Family: an institution designed by God to reveal who He is and to subdue and cultivate the world He has made.

What role would Abraham's family play in fulfilling God's promises?

How did God's promises, fulfilled through Abraham's family, reveal God's character?

"Become a great and mighty nation . . ."
"All the nations of the earth shall be blessed in him . . ."
"Command his children . . ."

This is family language. Which must have made little sense to Abraham's ears when he first heard the promise.

Why not according to Genesis 16:1, 17:17, and 18:11?

Everyone knows that to have descendants you have to continue the family line. To command your children, *you have to have children*. This was a covenant based on God's promises, which He always keeps.

Record what happened in Genesis 21:1–7.

Close the baby book. Our patriarchal couple got their happy ending. Except, when we read the whole Bible, we see that this family's story includes slave ownership, bitter jealousy, deception, sibling rivalry, and layer upon layer of sin. This should cause us to ask: **Why *did* God choose Abraham as the recipient of such a spiritually significant promise? What do you think?**

Now is a good time to remind you that we don't study the Bible merely to learn about the characters within it. We study the Bible to seek to understand the character of God.

Look up the following passages. Write down what each one reveals about God's promises.

Numbers 23:19

Joshua 21:45

Hebrews 10:23

God's promises are never built on man's worthiness, but on God's character and plan. Put a different way, God didn't pledge to bless Abraham's family because Abraham or his family were perfect, but to prove that *He* is.

Read Hebrews 6:13–20.

According to this passage, why should God's faithfulness to Abraham give us hope?

Think about your own family right now. Are there any circumstances that make you feel like God's promises can't be for you? Write them down.

How does Abraham's story reframe your perspective? Be specific.

In each lesson for this Week, you'll add details to Joseph's family tree. Fill in Abraham and Sarah in slots X and Y on the tree below.

WEEK 2 | DAY 2

TEACH US TO PRAY

Big Idea: *The needs within your family are an opportunity to reach toward the One who meets your needs.*

READ GENESIS 24–25

Though my children will make countless decisions over the course of their lives, two carry maximum weight in my thoughts and prayers:

1. Will they choose to follow Jesus?
2. Whom will they marry?

Obviously only one choice is of eternal significance, but both will have a profound impact on the trajectory of their lives.

Father Abraham knew this to be true for his own son of promise. Genesis 24 finds Abraham in his sunset years. He'd already buried his wife Sarah in the soil of Canaan. He knew his sons would soon be planning *his* funeral. As he considered his legacy, he urgently longed for Isaac to marry wisely and add faithful branches to the family tree.

Review Genesis 24:1–9.

Write down the specific instructions Abraham gave to his servant.

Pay close attention to verse 3. Why do you think Abraham was so adamant that his daughter-in-law should not be a Canaanite?

We are better able to understand the individual snapshots recorded in Scripture when we've studied enough to get the big picture. As we consider the Canaanites, again we see the impact of families. The Canaanites were a wicked people group descended from Noah's grandson, Canaan (Gen. 9:18). As part of His promise to Abraham and Abraham's descendants, God committed to drive all of the Canaanites out of the land (Ex. 33:2).

Abraham didn't want his son to take a wife from the land filled with pagan idol worshippers. He worked to intentionally preserve a family line of faith.

Review Genesis 24:1–9 below. This time circle every reference to God.

> Now Abraham was old, well advanced in years. And the Lord had blessed
> Abraham in all things. **2** And Abraham said to his servant, the oldest of his
> household, who had charge of all that he had, "Put your hand under my
> thigh, **3** that I may make you swear by the Lord, the God of heaven and
> God of the earth, that you will not take a wife for my son from the daughters
> of the Canaanites, among whom I dwell, **4** but will go to my country and
> to my kindred, and take a wife for my son Isaac." **5** The servant said to him,
> "Perhaps the woman may not be willing to follow me to this land. Must I
> then take your son back to the land from which you came?" **6** Abraham said
> to him, "See to it that you do not take my son back there. **7** The Lord, the
> God of heaven, who took me from my father's house and from the land of my
> kindred, and who spoke to me and swore to me, 'To your offspring I will give
> this land,' he will send his angel before you, and you shall take a wife for my
> son from there. **8** But if the woman is not willing to follow you, then you will
> be free from this oath of mine; only you must not take my son back there."
> **9** So the servant put his hand under the thigh of Abraham his master and
> swore to him concerning this matter.

Abraham didn't settle for doing what was best for himself or even what seemed best for his children in the moment. He sought to build a family that gave maximum glory and honor to God.

Think about the messages concerning family you receive from culture. According to the commercials, social media posts, movies, and shows you watch, what should be the goal of family life?

How does this look different, practically, from building a family with the mission of giving God maximum glory?

Write down the servant's prayer recorded in Genesis 24:12–14.

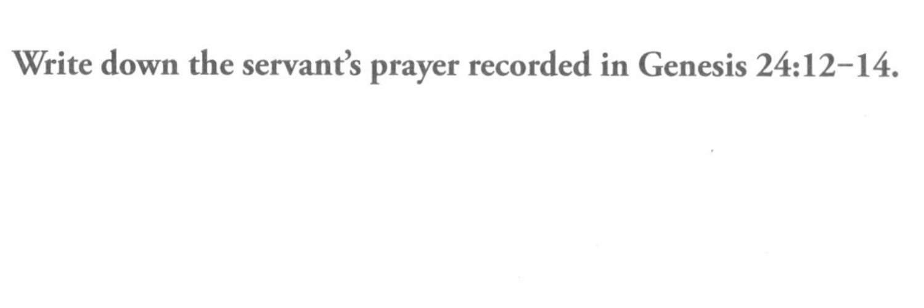

Is there someone in your family who needs God to provide something or someone for their future? Rewrite the servant's prayer in your own words.

The Lord heard the prayers of both Abraham and his servant. Genesis 24:62–67 records the beginning of the next generation of this family of promise.

> Now Isaac had returned from Beer-lahai-roi and was dwelling in the Negeb.
> **63** And Isaac went out to meditate in the field toward evening. And he lifted
> up his eyes and saw, and behold, there were camels coming. **64** And Rebekah
> lifted up her eyes, and when she saw Isaac, she dismounted from the camel
> **65** and said to the servant, "Who is that man, walking in the field to meet us?"
> The servant said, "It is my master." So she took her veil and covered herself.
> **66** And the servant told Isaac all the things that he had done. **67** Then Isaac
> brought her into the tent of Sarah his mother and took Rebekah, and she became
> his wife, and he loved her. So Isaac was comforted after his mother's death.

Sigh. Young love. But like in my family, and in yours, just because Isaac and Rebekah's family started out beautifully doesn't mean everything went smoothly.

According to Genesis 25:21, what major challenge did this young couple face?

How did Isaac respond? (v. 21)

Isaac's momma (Sarah) had trouble getting pregnant. Isaac's wife (Rebekah) had trouble getting pregnant. Though it's God's good design, family rarely just happens.

It's easy to look at others and think that their family is perfect. Perhaps they married young and had children effortlessly. No infertility. No miscarriages. Or you know of other families whose adult children all seem to be walking closely with the Lord. As you hang their Christmas card on the mantel you can't help but wonder, "Why is my child a prodigal?"

In these ancient marriages recorded in Scripture, and in our modern families, we see that *there are no perfect families.* Our very nature has been changed by sin (Gal. 5:17–25), and we must all live and raise our families in a world that is broken. That doesn't mean God's design is flawed. *It means we are flawed* and desperately need the Lord's help.

Abraham prayed for his son to find a wife. Isaac prayed for his wife to have a child. Their family stories teach us that the needs within our families are opportunities to reach toward the one who ultimately meets our needs—God. Praying for the members of your household is one way you can follow the positive example of the patriarchs.

As you wrap up today's study, use the prompts below to evaluate the impact of prayer on your family.

Is there anyone in your family whose commitment to prayer has made a significant difference in your life?

What kinds of things do/did they pray for?

What are the top three most pressing needs in your family right now?

Write out a game plan to pray for these areas more specifically and consistently.

Before you go, fill in the next section in Joseph's family tree. Place Isaac's name next to the X below and Rebekah's name next to the Y.

WEEK 2 | DAY 3

FAMILY FEUDS

Big idea: *Resist the urge to perpetually long for a different kind of family.*

READ GENESIS 25:19–34, 29–31

We may have a long-standing TV game show that says otherwise, but family feuds are far from entertaining. Whether it's sisters who refuse to speak to one another, children who have gone "no contact" with their parents, or factions within an extended family that take sides and draw hard lines, sometimes our families expose the very worst of our sin nature.

Are there any significant feuds in your family? Write about them below.

Do you see evidence that God is at work in these fractures? What would you like to see Him do?

Rebekah did receive the pregnancy news she longed for. **Review Genesis 25:22–23. What did the Lord reveal about the babies in Rebekah's womb?**

That's not the comforting thought a new mother wants to hear, but yet again, we see that God can do something significant through a broken family.

Using Genesis 25:24–28, compare and contrast Isaac and Rebekah's sons using the chart below.

	Esau	Jacob
Birth order		
Appearance		
Temperament		
Treatment by the family		

Next to Jacob's name in your Bible there is likely a footnote. Mine states, "Jacob means *He takes by the heel*, or *He cheats*."[4] As this story unfolds, we see that Jacob was born a cheater, and a cheater he did stay.

You'll have to read Genesis 27 to see the twins' young adult years. It involves a bowl of stew, hairy arms, a mom who played favorites, and high-stakes sibling rivalry—so much so that it caused the family to split down the middle.

Record Genesis 27:41 below.

I don't think my brother, whose name ironically is Jacob, has ever put me on a hit list. So, my family is one step ahead of this one. But I need to keep reminding us of something. This is the family of Abraham through which God promised all the nations of the world would be blessed. I *need* you to see that it was surely not because they were a perfect family that always honored Him. They weren't. God used them anyway.

Does this fact give you hope? Explain your answer.

Because of the family split, Jacob ran away from his ancestral home and came to the tent of a man named Laban. As you already read, Laban had two daughters: Rachel and Leah. Rachel was so beautiful that Jacob wept when he kissed her (Gen. 29:11). Eat your heart out, Hallmark. Except . . . Jacob got tricked into marrying Rachel's less desirable sister, Leah. Then he married Rachel too. And right there in the pages of our Bible we see marriages built on deception and filled with a great deal of hurt.

Again, consider your own family. Have there been any specific marriages in your family line that have brought extra sorrow? How about those that have brought extra blessing?

If you're married, what impact do you hope your marriage has on future generations? Be specific.

Review Genesis 29:30–31. What longings do you think Leah had?

Like Leah, are there circumstances in your family that exacerbate your craving to be loved? In my case, it's a deep wound cut into my heart by my father's estrangement when I was a little girl and the continued reality of that estrangement so many years later. I understand Leah's longing. I bet there's a part of you that does too.

Review Genesis 30:1–2. What longings did Rachel have?

Like Rachel, are there things you yearn for your family that God has not granted? A healthy pregnancy? A believing husband? A reconciled relationship?

What we see in Rachel and Leah is that they didn't get the family they longed for. Leah had to live without a husband who only had eyes for her. Temporarily, Rachel didn't get a womb filled with the babies she longed to hold. Neither of them got a relationship with their sister that provided comfort from the many demands of life.

Genesis 30 is fraught with dysfunction. It records that the sisters were always fighting over who got to sleep with their shared husband. They kept pushing their servants toward him so he could have sex with them too and give them children. Yuck. But this is also the chapter where we finally see Joseph.

Read Genesis 30:22–24. What does the Bible record about Joseph's birth?

Joseph's name means "he will add."[5] Even as she held her first baby boy in her arms, Rachel was still longing for a different kind of family. This fact begs for us to pause and apply what we're learning.

Jump out of Genesis for a moment to Psalm 84:11. What promise is given here?

To be fair, this is not always a comfortable truth to apply. When you long for a godly husband, it can be difficult to understand why your spouse's heart remains hard. When you ache for a baby, it can be painful to grasp why God hasn't yet granted that request. The Lord's shoulders are wide enough to handle our wrestling with such painful realities, but we can also learn to trust that the family we have has been filtered through the loving hands of a generous God. This frees us from the turmoil our foremothers must have experienced as they chronically longed for a different kind of family.

Which of your family circumstances have you most struggled to be content with?

Write out a prayer of repentance and ask the Lord to help you avoid the patterns of Rachel and Leah.

Joseph's birth didn't put an end to all the infighting. Another family feud erupted, this time between Jacob and his father-in-law. (Yes, the Bible talks about in-law relationships too.) This fracture sent Jacob running back to his hometown. Genesis 32 records the sweet moment that Jacob and his brother Esau were reconciled, and there's an important nugget embedded in the text.

Write out Genesis 32:28 below.

"Israel." Wow. Ring any bells?

God really was birthing something special. A family—from Abraham's family—that stands unique among the families of the world (though that's going to take several more generations).

Though not every family heartache ends with a happy ending, the story of the brothers who had warred since the womb does.

Read Genesis 33.

How do you see God's redemptive plan at work in this chapter of the story?

Jacob spoke powerful blessings to his brother when they reunited.

Write down what he said as recorded in Genesis 33:11 below.

Look again. What motivated Jacob to be generous toward the brother he'd been estranged from for so long?

What a contrast! The brothers split because Rebekah wanted more for one son than he currently had. The sisters fought because they wanted more than God had given them. Yet here we see healing and wholeness brought to a family as one brother said, "God has dealt graciously with me" and "I have enough."

What if it's not the circumstances of our families that most need to be changed, but our attitudes? And what if our hearts don't first need to be reoriented toward our children and siblings, but first and foremost need to be reoriented toward God? What if contentment, based on the goodness and faithfulness of God, is the salve our fractured families need most?

To wrap up today's study, meditate on 1 Timothy 6:6–8 by doodling it below. Then add to Joseph's family tree by adding Jacob, Rachel, and Leah to lines X and Y.

But godliness with contentment is great gain,
for we brought nothing into the world,
and we cannot take anything out of the world.
But if we have food and clothing,
with these we will be content.

WEEK 2 | DAY 4

THE DEFILING OF DINAH

Big Idea: *God's Word speaks to our darkest family moments.*

READ GENESIS 34–35

Sometimes saying family is messy is akin to saying "it's sprinkling" in the middle of a hurricane. Some family drama moves beyond the painful to the truly desperate.

Joseph's family has some of those stories, branches on the family tree so gnarled by sin and wickedness we'd prefer not to see them at all. But since the inspired Word of God chooses not to look away, neither will we, not for the sake of mere sensationalism, but in order to apply hope to the darkest parts of our family stories.

According to Genesis 34:1, whose daughter was Dinah?

How is Dinah related to Joseph?

Born into a loveless marriage in a highly dysfunctional family, Dinah surely faced challenges from the start. And then . . . a trauma no woman should know.

According to Genesis 34:2, what three things did Shechem do to Dinah?

This was a man of power (v. 2), clearly accustomed to getting what he wanted. He didn't just want Dinah once. He wanted her as his property forever. He went to his father and demanded, "Get me this girl for my wife" (v. 4).

Freeze frame. Let's consider what would have happened if Shechem's dad had been righteous. What if he had prioritized honoring God over the demands of his spoiled son? That would be the end of the story. I doubt the Spirit would preserve it in His Word for us to read centuries later. But that's not who Shechem's dad was. God's will clearly wasn't what he wanted.

What did Shechem's father, Hamor, suggest to Jacob in Genesis 34:9–10?

Why was this a bad idea?

Hamor had more in mind than getting his son the bride that he begged for. Likely seeing God's favor on Jacob and his sons, Hamor hatched a bigger plan. He wanted to intermarry the children of Jacob with the daughters of the land. We can draw a pretty straight line from this passage to the ones we read in Genesis 3. Satan seeks to undo God's good plan for families. I imagine the serpent was behind the temptation for Jacob to veer from the set-apart family line God promised to Abraham by intermarrying with the pagan families of Canaan.

The sons of Jacob responded to Hamor's request by asking for the entire opposing tribe to be circumcised. Do you think their intent was righteous? Defend your answer. (Hint: verse 13.)

With the rival men in a weakened state (try to imagine the recovery from ancient circumcision), Dinah's brothers sought vengeance for their sister. What did they do according to Genesis 34:25–29?

Is there evidence in the text that God commanded the brothers to do this?

Did they act righteously? Explain your answer.

Pay close attention to Genesis 34:29. What does this reveal about the brothers' character?

This information will come in handy as Joseph's story unfolds. The kind of men who will hurt little ones will also throw their brother in a pit and lie to cover it up.

Violence.
Trauma.
Deceit.
Sexual sin and abuse.

These all water the roots of Joseph's family tree. To one degree or another, they water the roots of all our family trees. Dinah's story isn't recorded in Scripture just so we can commiserate with the pain of sin's destructive pathway through our families, but so that when we get to God's redemption in this story—in our stories—we see just how much He can redeem us from.

Dinah's story doesn't get tied up in a tidy bow in the chapters of Genesis. Some of the most broken parts of your family won't either, not this side of heaven. Neither is God oblivious to the truly painful parts of our family stories. He sees. He cares. He is working to redeem.

Review Genesis 35:1–15. What did God command Jacob to do? (v. 1)

Who did Jacob take with him to Bethel? (vv. 2–3)

What command did God repeat? (v. 11)

Where have you read that command before?

What promise did God reiterate? (v. 12)

We've just flown through the first half of the first book of the Bible and we've already seen a pattern repeated:

- God establishes families for man's good and His glory.
- Sin fractures those families.
- God redeems.
- Repeat. Repeat. Repeat.

The snake tried to destroy the first family. Instead, God confirmed His plan for Adam and Eve to be fruitful and multiply.

The serpent tried again with the family of Abraham. Certainly, sin left pock marks on the hearts and lives of this family of promise. And yet, God confirmed His plan: "Be fruitful and multiply" (Gen. 1:28).

God established a family for man's good and His glory.
Sin fractured that family.
God redeemed.
Repeat. Repeat. Repeat.

God had a plan, a generational plan. God *has* a plan, a generational plan.

Sin is never without consequences. If your family has experienced some of the horrors Dinah's did, you already know that is true. **But no sin can dethrone God, and no sin is beyond His redemption.**

As you wrap up today's study, meditate on Psalm 107. It's a song about what God can do, even in the face of destruction. **Then add Dinah's name to Joseph's family tree.** She wasn't just the daughter of a couple with a complex marriage. She is more than an assault victim. She's a sister. She's a child of God. She has a family. **Place Dinah's name on spot X on Joseph's family tree.**

X
Jacob
Rachel and Leah
Isaac
Rebekah
Abraham
Sarah

WEEK 2 | DAY 5

LEAVE A LEGACY OF PRAYER

You can have a profound influence on your family by developing the discipline of prayer. **Take time today to intercede for your family. Use the prompts below as a guide.**

Write down the names of the family members you want to pray for today. Next to each name, write down one need you want to see God meet.

Are there patterns of sin and brokenness that you need God to interrupt? Make a list and pray through it.

What can you praise God for about your family today?

What generational work do you want to see God do in your family? Write it out as a prayer.

Write out Isaiah 41:10 as a prayer of blessing for your family.

Playing Favorites

what:

The favoritism in Joseph's family reflects a bigger story.

so what?

See the gospel in Joseph's story and relish your chosen status.

The tiny church was packed with mourners with teary eyes and black clothing. Well into his nineties, my Pop (grandpa) was beloved. None of us were quite ready to say goodbye.

With a lump in my throat, I stepped up to the microphone. Flanked by siblings, cousins, and aunts and uncles, I announced, "I was Pop's favorite."

No one rolled their eyes. We had an understanding: we *all* felt like we were Pop's favorite. All three of his daughters and all six of his grandchildren (me included) experienced Pop's adoration and bloomed under it.

WEEK 3

Of course, I've also experienced the opposite. There are family members who prefer someone else's company over my own. I've felt the sting of knowing that someone else is more liked and understood than I am. You've felt it too. That doesn't mean your family is especially broken, just that it is made up of sinners in desperate need of a Savior.

In this way, and in so many others, Joseph's experience with family is much like our own. In this session, you'll see how a coat can divide brothers and how one father's favoritism tells the story of *the* Father's favoritism. (Hint: You are the apple of His eye.)

Open your Bible to Genesis 37. Let Joseph's story point you to God's bigger story—the gospel story.

WEEK 3 | DAY 1

A FATHER'S FAVORITE

Big Idea: *Sin has a profound and disastrous effect on every family.*

READ GENESIS 37

As we pick up Joseph's story, he has grown from a baby boy to a young man. His mother Rachel was dead, and his father Jacob was raising his family in the ancestral homeland where *his* father Isaac had lived, and where his grandfather Abraham had pitched his tent in obedience to God's call.

According to Genesis 37:2, what's one of the things Moses, the author of Genesis, wanted to capture with his writings?

I hope that one outcome of this study is that we will stop glossing over family language in the pages of our Bibles. It's everywhere! Among other things, it communicates God's care for our families and His work across generations.

According to verse 2, what did Joseph do to his brothers?

Why do you think Scripture records this detail?

Joseph wasn't just a tattler. He was also a dreamer.

Review Genesis 37:5–11. Which attitudes would have been logical for the brothers to ascribe to Joseph after he reported his dreams? Circle all that apply.

Arrogance	Humility	Cockiness	Superiority
Gracefulness	Zeal	Deference	Leadership

What word does verse 8 use to describe how the brothers felt toward Joseph?

At this point in the story, do you feel Joseph had earned their hatred? Explain.

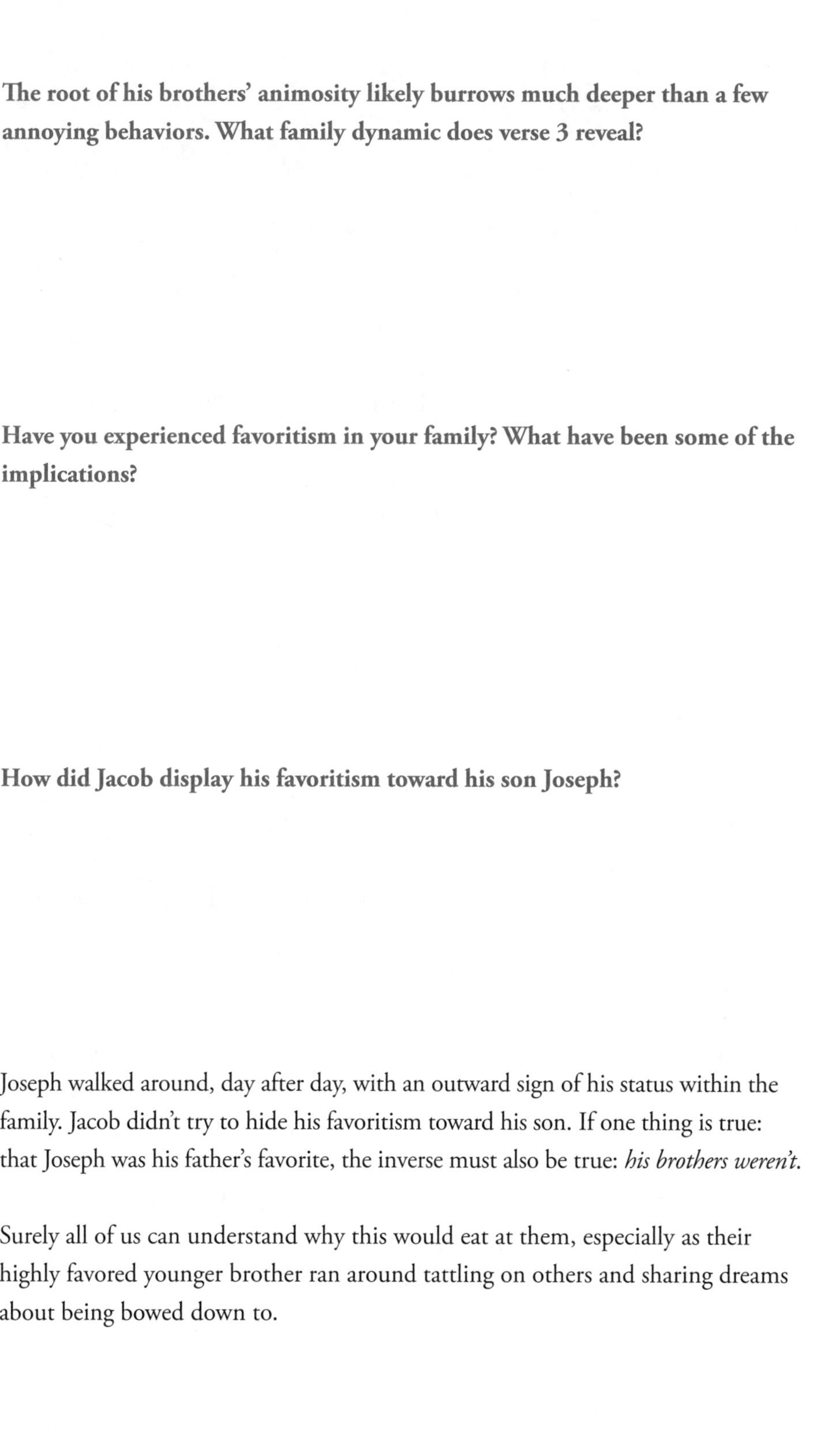

The root of his brothers' animosity likely burrows much deeper than a few annoying behaviors. What family dynamic does verse 3 reveal?

Have you experienced favoritism in your family? What have been some of the implications?

How did Jacob display his favoritism toward his son Joseph?

Joseph walked around, day after day, with an outward sign of his status within the family. Jacob didn't try to hide his favoritism toward his son. If one thing is true: that Joseph was his father's favorite, the inverse must also be true: *his brothers weren't.*

Surely all of us can understand why this would eat at them, especially as their highly favored younger brother ran around tattling on others and sharing dreams about being bowed down to.

It's tempting to point fingers.

- Israel caused the issue by choosing favorites . . .
- Joseph caused the issue by being insensitive . . .
- The brothers caused the issue by letting their annoyance and jealousy metastasize to hate . . .

. . . but these are just symptoms of a sickness that all of us suffer from. Let's use the rest of this Week to develop a theology of sin.

How do you define sin? Write your definition below.

Fill in the blank for 1 John 3:4: "Everyone who makes a practice of sinning also practices lawlessness; sin is ______________________."

This verse isn't strictly referencing human law, but rather God's law. These are the commands given by God in His Word to regulate our lives. Since the Bible covers God's intention for our thoughts and behaviors, we can know that sin is deeper than what we do or don't do. Sin is first and foremost a condition of our hearts.

James 1:14–15 describes the disastrous progression sin always takes. Look up this verse and fill in the steps below.

Sin Step 1: Enticed by _______________

↓

Sin Step 2: Desire gives birth to _______________

↓

Sin Step 3: Sin always brings _______________

Sin is serious. Deadly serious.

According to Romans 3:23, how many of us have sinned?

Every member of your family is a sinner. From the widdlest baby to the greyest-haired grandpa.

What does Romans 5:12 reveal about sin?

Adam's sin has been passed to all people in every generation since the garden. Sin goes well beyond something we do, it's our nature (Eph. 4:22). **Our pervasive and persistent sin problem has a profound effect on our families.**

Recognizing the results of sin in our families can be overwhelming, but it also helps us aim at the right target. Instead of fighting against each other, we can rightly square our sites at Satan, the one who tempts us toward sin while seeking to take our families down.

To wrap up today's study, fill in the blank for Ephesians 6:12–13 below. In the blank below where the Bible text would say "flesh and blood," write the names of some of your family members as a reminder that the ultimate battle our families are fighting is the one against sin.

> For we do not wrestle against ______________________________,
> but against the rulers, against the authorities, against the cosmic powers over this present darkness, against the spiritual forces of evil in the heavenly places. Therefore take up the whole armor of God, that you may be able to withstand in the evil day, and having done all, to stand firm. (Eph. 6:12–13)

WEEK 3 | DAY 2

YOUR FAMILY IS A MISSIONARY

Big Idea: *God wants to use your family to showcase your need for a Savior.*

READ ROMANS 1:18–32

One of the (many) things I hate about my sinfulness is the ways it hurts those I love most. My husband and sons, my parents, my siblings . . . they're all walking around with shrapnel in their hearts because of my sin. Your family members have sin shrapnel too. It's easier to focus on the ways our family members' sin has hurt *us*. (That's part of the way sin warps our perspective.) Yet, the Bible is ever calling us to humbly acknowledge *our* sin before focusing on the sin of others.

Perhaps we can see why if we use our creative imaginations with Joseph's story. What if Jacob had obsessed over the seething anger of his older sons? What if the brothers prayed night and day for God to pour out His wrath on Joseph for his juvenile tattling? What if Joseph yelled at his brothers, "Well, I wouldn't act like such a brat if you didn't hate me"? This kind of stalemate is far too common and rarely (if ever) moves us toward the redemptive path God has for us.

Part of embracing God's good design for family is recognizing the ways being part of a family exposes our true condition. Perhaps you've thought, "I never had an issue with anger until I had kids and had to go without sleep for months on end!" In truth, the Lord has used the circumstances of your family to expose a short fuse that always existed in your heart.

Here's another example. You and your husband are locked into a pattern of arguments. You think (and perhaps say), "I wouldn't need to fight with him if he just did what I asked!"

James 4:2 offers an uncomfortable alternative to this idea. According to this verse, why do you fight with others?

Look up Exodus 20:12. Why did God need to literally carve this idea into stone? I mean, don't we all naturally want to honor and obey our parents? (That was sarcasm.)

Our families provide unique opportunities to see our depravity. We snap instead of speaking life. We withhold forgiveness though we've been freely forgiven. We seek to manipulate and control rather than love our family members as they are. Though we can (and do!) sin in other spheres of our lives such as work and friendship, family works like a super bright bulb, exposing the sin that exists in each of us.

Has God used your family to expose your sinful patterns of thinking and acting? Explain.

Joseph's brothers' sin didn't fizzle out on its own. It evolved and grew, moving from annoyance, to hatred, to violence and thoughts of murder.

Review Romans 1:28–32 below. Underline anything that could be used to describe Joseph's brothers.

> **28** And since they did not see fit to acknowledge God, God gave them up to
> a debased mind to do what ought not to be done. **29** They were filled with all
> manner of unrighteousness, evil, covetousness, malice. They are full of envy,
> murder, strife, deceit, maliciousness. They are gossips, **30** slanderers, haters
> of God, insolent, haughty, boastful, inventors of evil, disobedient to parents,
> **31** foolish, faithless, heartless, ruthless. **32** Though they know God's righteous
> decree that those who practice such things deserve to die, they not only do
> them but give approval to those who practice them.

Our families are in constant risk of these same disastrous consequences. God could rightly turn us over to our wrong ways of thinking and behaving, which would entrench us into deep pits of sin. Instead, He uses our families to expose our sinfulness so that we can turn from it and find freedom. *In this way, your family is a missionary, ever exposing your desperate need for a Savior.*

Joseph's brothers knew there was a God. They knew His name (Gen. 42:28). They knew His promise. But the Lord used their little brother to expose their evil desires: They wanted to be the favored ones, and their pride roared in protest when that wasn't the case. Once exposed, any of the brothers could have responded with repentance and run toward the Lord. They didn't—not one. What a spectacular mess their sin made!

Write out 1 John 1:9–10 below.

God is no liar (Titus 1:2; Heb. 6:18). You really do have a sin problem. But you also have a Savior, willing to forgive and redeem your sin and its impact on your family.

To wrap up today's lesson, move into a time of confession. Ask the Lord to show you how your sin has left a mark on your family. Then repent and ask Him to help you turn away from sin and run toward righteousness.

Lord, I repent of . . . .

WEEK 3 | DAY 3

GOD'S FAVORITE FAVORED PEOPLE

Big Idea: *The details of Joseph's story declare the beauty of the gospel.*

READ EXODUS 19:4–6

We often try to read our modern, Western context into Bible stories that are neither modern nor Western.

We've been trained to think that parents shouldn't play favorites, and certainly that has some biblical backing (more on that in a moment). But we see several examples in Scripture where some children were entitled to gifts that not all the children were. When we miss that, we also miss the overarching redemptive story that God reveals through His Word. The problem is actually more systemic than that. We tend to study and teach the individual stories preserved in Scripture as the main idea and God's redemptive plan as the sub-theme when the reverse is true. The Bible is proclaiming the Big Story of God's dramatic redemption and simply using many different little stories to do it. Joseph's story is no exception.

THE BIBLE IS PROCLAIMING THE BIG STORY OF GOD'S DRAMATIC REDEMPTION AND SIMPLY USING MANY DIFFERENT LITTLE STORIES TO DO IT. JOSEPH'S STORY IS NO EXCEPTION.

Attempt to set your modern, Western context aside and face this fact, which is crystal clear in the text: Joseph was his father's favorite son. He was highly favored above many other sons.

Based on what you've learned so far, why do you think Joseph was Jacob's favorite?

Did you write down Jacob's love for Rachel? Remember that he wept when he kissed her and worked many long years to marry her. Maybe Joseph looked like his mom and reminded his dad of the woman he missed. Did you note that Joseph was the child of Jacob's old age? We do grow more sentimental as the years pass, don't we?

None of these were circumstances chosen by Joseph. He didn't ask to be his dad's favorite, nor did he earn it. The coat his father gifted him represented many things, among them unmerited favor.

Review Exodus 19:4–6 in your Bible. Record the words God uses to describe the nation of Israel (v. 5).

Though God made all the peoples of the earth, He has a favorite. These words were spoken to Abraham's descendants—*to Joseph's descendants*—the nation of Israel. Remember Jacob's new name? His twelve sons, who we will learn to love and hate as Joseph's story unfolds, would birth the twelve tribes of a nation, *a chosen nation.* Here in Exodus 19, and many (many!) times elsewhere in Scripture, God announced His favoritism toward them. It was not something they earned or deserved. It was unmerited favor.

Read Deuteronomy 7:6–10 below. Underline the phrase repeated from Exodus 19. Circle the reasons why God chose Israel as His treasured possession.

> **6** For you are a people holy to the LORD your God. The LORD your God has
> chosen you to be a people for his treasured possession, out of all the peoples who
> are on the face of the earth. **7** It was not because you were more in number
> than any other people that the LORD set his love on you and chose you, for
> you were the fewest of all peoples, **8** but it is because the LORD loves you and is
> keeping the oath that he swore to your fathers, that the LORD has brought you
> out with a mighty hand and redeemed you from the house of slavery, from the
> hand of Pharaoh king of Egypt. **9** Know therefore that the LORD your God is
> God, the faithful God who keeps covenant and steadfast love with those who
> love him and keep his commandments, to a thousand generations, **10** and
> repays to their face those who hate him, by destroying them. He will not be
> slack with one who hates him. He will repay him to his face.

In both His favoritism toward Israel and in the story of Joseph, God is telling the same story. *He is telling His story.* He is telling *our* story.

Read Galatians 3:13–14. According to this passage, who does God's blessing of redemption extend to (v. 14)?

Because of Jesus, God's favor extends beyond His favorite child, Israel, to us—t he other brothers, so to speak. The parallels don't stop there. There is a robe that unifies us, rather than dividing us.

How does Revelation 19:13 describe this robe?

What color is this robe? What do you think that signifies?

Jesus died for all sinners, not just the Israelites, and certainly not just those who deserved it, as none of us deserve God's grace. Yet Christ made a way for all to be reconciled to Him. One of the reasons we open our Bibles again and again is because there is value in understanding God's long history of dealing with broken people and broken families in ways that show off His unmerited favor toward us.

This is the gospel! If we want our families to flourish, we must build them on this granite foundation.

Read James 2:1–9. What does this passage teach us about favoritism?

How do you reconcile this with God's clear favoritism toward the nation of Israel?

The gospel obliterates favoritism because the ground is level at the cross. *We all need Jesus.* Our family life begins to change when this is the foundation upon which we build our views of each other because knowing this oozes out of our pores in the form of humility. Humility is the great destroyer of favoritism.

To wrap up today's study, make a list of your family members. Next to each name write the words "needs Jesus." Put your name at the top of the list.

WEEK 3 | DAY 4

YOU'RE HIS FAVORITE

Big Idea: *You're God's favorite.*

READ EPHESIANS 1:3–6

Have you experienced being the favorite of someone in your family? Write about it below.

Have you experienced *not* being the favorite in your family? Write about it below.

Maybe you look around your family gatherings and all you see are coats of many colors—signs of favoritism—and you don't seem to have one. Perhaps, more tragically, you get that same sensation among the family of God. *She* has gifts that you don't. *He* has been blessed by God in ways that seem so obvious.

Family life makes it difficult to hide our insecurities. Have you paused to wonder: What if that's by design?

I heard the story once of a woman who received a letter from her dad. He had written it from his deathbed, sealed it in an envelope, then had it dropped in the mail for her to receive after his death. He wrote about his deep love for his daughter, then told her something he asked her not to share with her brothers and sisters. "You're my favorite," he wrote. "You've always been my favorite."

The woman carried that sentiment in her heart for many years. There's profound assurance that comes from knowing that someone picked *you* as the focus of their adoration.

Until one day, in a family conversation, another sibling let it slip that he was their dad's favorite. He knew because Dad had written to him from his deathbed letting him know, "You're my favorite. You've always been my favorite."

The jig was up. He had written a similar letter to each of his children. Part of his legacy was leaving them with the hope that they were definitively and uniquely loved.

The story of Joseph is not fictional. It really happened, but it is also a picture of God's love for you. Through His Word, our Father has sent a letter. In it He expresses His supernatural love for you.

Review Ephesians 1:3–6 below. Underline when He chose you (v. 4). Circle why He predestined you to be adopted into His forever family (v. 4).

> 3 Blessed be the God and Father of our Lord Jesus Christ, who has blessed
> us in Christ with every spiritual blessing in the heavenly places, 4 even as he
> chose us in him before the foundation of the world, that we should be holy
> and blameless before him. In love 5 he predestined us for adoption to himself
> as sons through Jesus Christ, according to the purpose of his will, 6 to the
> praise of his glorious grace, with which he has blessed us in the Beloved.

These words were written long before you took your first breath. Before you had the chance to do a single thing to impress God or commit a single sin to disappoint Him, He declared His intention to adopt you as His child. Like Joseph, you are the blessed recipient of your Father's unmerited favor.

How does this line up with what you've learned about love from your family?

Read Jeremiah 31:1–3. How does God describe His love for Israel in verse 3?

What are some other ways to say that? Make a list.

Based on what you've learned about the gospel, is God's everlasting love available to you too? Explain.

Regardless of how your family members see you, you have a Father who loves you. Resting in this reality helps us navigate the complexities of life and family free of the compulsion to be the apple of everyone's eye. You can live secure in the Father's love, knowing that He chose you for His family before He even poured the foundations of the earth.

Wrap up today's study deeply comforted by this thought: **You're His favorite. You've always been His favorite.**

WEEK 3 | DAY 5

LEAVE A LEGACY OF PRAYER

You can have a profound influence on your family by developing the discipline of prayer. **Take time today to intercede for your family. Use the prompts below as a guide.**

Write down the names of the family members you want to pray for today. Next to each name, write down one need you want to see God meet.

Are there patterns of sin and brokenness that you need God to interrupt? Make a list and pray through it.

What can you praise God for about your family today?

What generational work do you want to see God do in your family? Write it out as a prayer.

Write out 3 John 1:2 as a prayer of blessing for your family.

Making Room for Mystery

what:

Each moment in your family life is just a snapshot.
God is doing infinitely more.

so what?

Acknowledge that your view is limited.
Trust God with what you can't see yet.

One of the things we've lost to the digital age are family photo albums. Sure, we can scroll through pictures on our phone or look through our memories on social media, but it's not the same as holding an actual photo album in your lap, turning the pages with your mom or grandma and listening as she narrates the snapshots of your life.

As we move forward systematically through the story of Joseph, we come to a snapshot that no family wants in their album. Undercurrents of jealousy and bitterness swell into a raging river that sweeps Joseph from the arms of his father and away from his ancestral home. Ah, but it's just a snapshot. God was at work. God is always at work.

As you study this week, you'll be pressed to lean hard into God's providence, to trust that He is doing more than you can think or imagine regarding your family. And that's not even the best part—Joseph's little story points us to the Bigger Story of Jesus and what He did to redeem *all* things.

It's time to **open your Bible** once again. Let's linger in Genesis 37, asking God to expand our vision and to trust He is always doing more than we can see.

WEEK 4 | DAY 1

SON OF A DREAMER

Big Idea: *Don't expect to understand everything God is doing in the story of your family.*

READ GENESIS 37:5–11

You're nearly halfway through this study, and we're still studying the chapter that records Joseph as a young man, herding sheep under the annoyed glances of his big brothers. Fear not, our study of Joseph's life will soon accelerate. But remember: our mission isn't to memorize the details of the life of one Bible character, nor is it strictly to understand our families better.

What is the purpose of Scripture? (The answer is in bold in the study's introduction.)

What's the first and best question for us to ask of any passage of the Bible?

Did you answer, "What does this tell me about God?" **What have you learned about the character and ways of God based on what you've studied so far in Joseph's story?**

Let's circle back to the dreams. Read Genesis 37:5–7. Summarize Joseph's dreams in your own words.

How did the brothers respond? (v. 8)

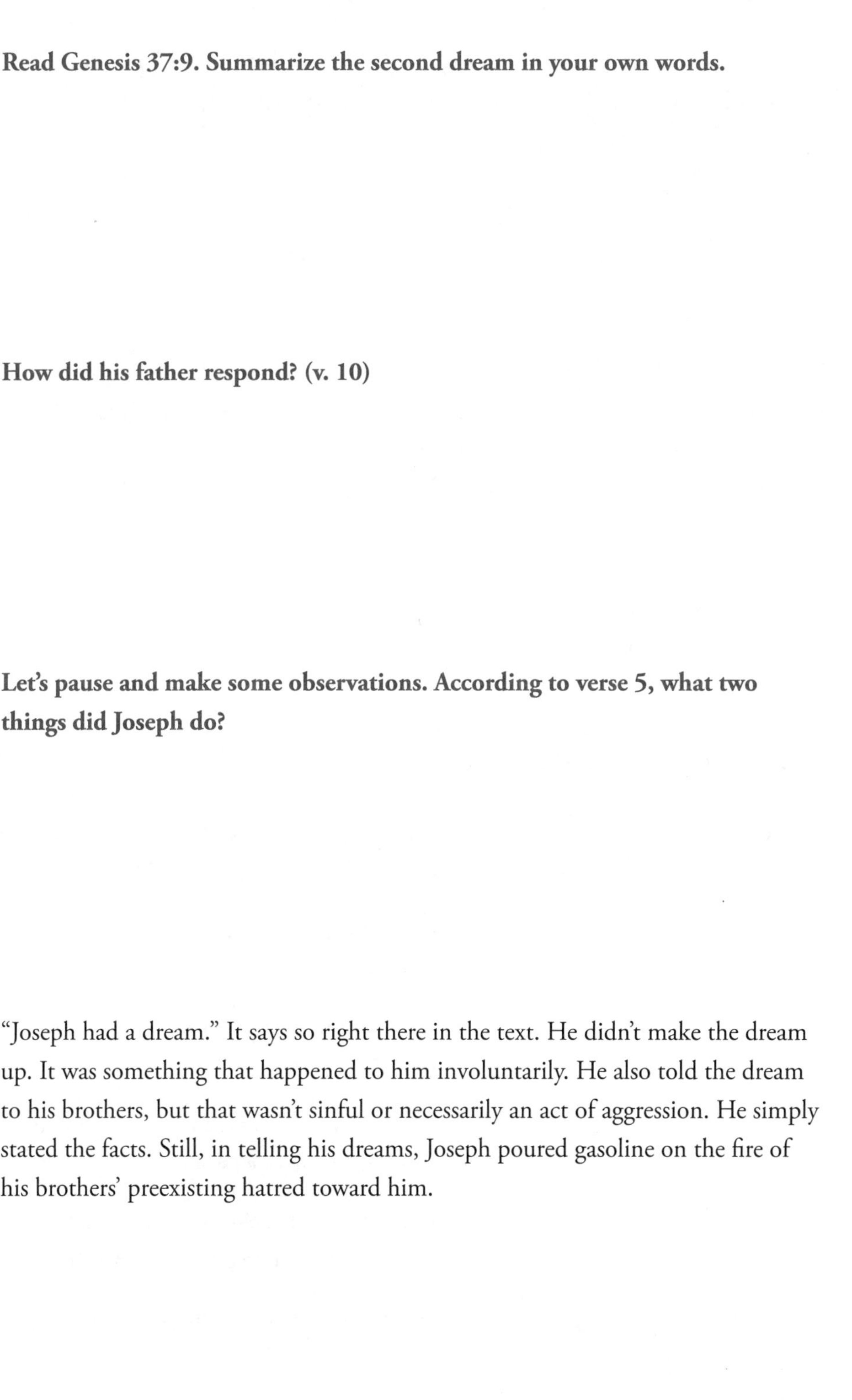

Read Genesis 37:9. Summarize the second dream in your own words.

How did his father respond? (v. 10)

Let's pause and make some observations. According to verse 5, what two things did Joseph do?

"Joseph had a dream." It says so right there in the text. He didn't make the dream up. It was something that happened to him involuntarily. He also told the dream to his brothers, but that wasn't sinful or necessarily an act of aggression. He simply stated the facts. Still, in telling his dreams, Joseph poured gasoline on the fire of his brothers' preexisting hatred toward him.

Consider your own sinful inclinations, then put yourself in the brothers' shoes. Why do you think Joseph's dreams were so upsetting to them?

There is a rebel inside each of us that hates the idea of anyone having power over us. Proverbs 16:18 warns that pride is a forerunner to destruction and, as we'll see, the brothers' pride is about to blow their family to smithereens. But the brothers aren't the main focus of these passages. Neither is Joseph. God was at work, accomplishing *His* purposes in the life of this chosen family.

Joseph's story reveals one obvious, though a bit unconventional, truth: Sometimes God works through dreams. In fact, to believe the Bible means to accept that God *often* works through dreams.

Match the passage with the correct statement below.

Daniel 1:17	God speaks in dreams when man is asleep in their beds.
Matthew 1:20–25	God helped Daniel understand the meaning of dreams.
Acts 2:16–18	At one time, God spoke to Saul through dreams.
Matthew 2:13–15	The Lord appeared to Joseph in a dream to reveal the coming Messiah.
Job 33:14–15	God appeared to Joseph in a dream a second time and told him to take Jesus to Egypt.
1 Samuel 28:15	Old men will dream dreams in the last days.

Does speaking through dreams line up with what you've been taught about how God works? Write down your thoughts on that.

Since our focus is on God's work through families, I won't take us far down that rabbit trail, but you do need to know that dreams play a significant role in the story of Joseph.

Flip back to Genesis 28:10–17 to find another dreamer in Joseph's family line. Whose dream is recorded here?

Summarize Jacob's dream in your own words.

Who did Jacob credit his dream to? (v. 16)

Joseph, it seems, was not the first in the family to receive a dream of supernatural significance. Jacob knew what it was like to receive a God-given dream.

Still, according to Genesis 37:10, what was Jacob's first reaction to his son's dreams?

What does Genesis 37:11 record that Jacob also did? What do you think this means?

Though Jacob had experienced the dream-giving power of God, He didn't fully understand or embrace it when God spoke through dreams to his son. This is just one more way Joseph's story may mirror your own.

Have you experienced a time when God was at work in your life and your family members struggled to understand and embrace it? Write about it below.

The reverse is likely also true. **Has there been a time when someone in your family had an experience with God or took a step of obedience to God that felt strange to you? How did you respond?**

What we see in Scripture is that when God calls someone to a step of obedience, He doesn't put up a billboard to alert everyone else to what's happening. Look back at the list of dreams above. God gave Daniel the ability to understand dreams, but didn't remove him from a godless culture. The Lord gave Jesus' father Joseph clear instructions in a dream, but Scripture gives no indication that the Spirit also took the time to explain Joseph's decision to his friends and family. God may work in supernatural ways in your life that your family may not understand, and God may work in supernatural ways in the lives of your family that you may not understand. When we try to make God's work fit our paradigm, we may find ourselves agitated and cynical, just like Joseph's brothers.

To bring this point home, let's jump from Joseph's story to the New Testament.

Look up John 21:18–22. What was Jesus' response to Peter's question, "Lord, what about this man?" (v. 21)?

Jesus was giving Peter important information about what would be required of him as a follower of Jesus. The news was not easy to hear, and Peter deflected by looking at John and asking essentially, "But what are you going to require of *this guy*?"

Jesus said, "What's that to you?" In other words, "My plans for John are none of your business." God had a specific message and calling for Peter, and He had a specific message and calling for John. Each man was responsible to listen and obey Jesus for himself.

Did you ever stop to wonder if Joseph's brothers received supernatural dreams? They were all part of the same family and recipients of the same promises from God. We don't know the answer to that question because the text doesn't tell us. But we can recognize the error of dismissing or rejecting God's work in the lives of those we love simply because we don't fully understand it.

Write down an alternate way Jacob and the brothers could have responded to Joseph's dream.

What difference would an openness to the movement of God have made in their family dynamic?

WEEK 4 | DAY 2

TWO KEYS

Big Idea: *Learn to see Scripture as a whole. Jesus is the key that unlocks the Bible.*

READ ROMANS 15:4

When French forces invaded Egypt under the leadership of Napoleon in 1798, they weren't looking to decode ancient languages. Still, soldiers discovered a large slab of stone inscribed with three languages. Named for the city in which it was found, the Rosetta Stone became one of the most important artifacts ever discovered because the languages inscribed on it made it possible to decode Egyptian hieroglyphics.[6] Weighing in at 1,676 pounds,[7] it would be hard to hang the Rosetta Stone on any key ring; still, it did unlock a world of information that dramatically shifted our understanding of the ancient world.

As we continue to dig into our Bibles, let's pause and marvel at the unique tools we've been given as modern children of God.

First, we have the entire canon of Scripture.

Though we haven't covered it yet in this study, if you've been in church long at all, you likely already know that Joseph's dreams did come true.

Write down what you know from memory. How and when did Joseph's brothers bow down to him?

Did God keep His promises to Abraham, Isaac, and Jacob? Be specific.

Abraham's people did go on to become a great nation and inhabit the fruitful land God promised them. And Joseph's brothers did bow before him (more on that soon). This is the beauty of knowing our whole Bible. We get to see the big picture in ways that the people on the pages never could—which brings us to some important hermeneutics (the interpretation of Scripture).

1. Every text is part of a context.

Every word in the Bible is part of a verse.

Every verse is part of a paragraph.

Every paragraph is part of a book.

Every book is part of the whole of Scripture.

No verse should be divided from the verses around it. No story should be separated from the rest of Scripture.

In your experience, what is the danger of extracting single verses or stories and trying to understand them outside of the wider context of the Bible?

2. We let Scripture interpret Scripture.

It is essential for us to interpret a passage in light of what the rest of Scripture says on the topic. A correct interpretation is always consistent with the rest of Scripture. Because of this, we study systematically, seeking to understand what God is saying *in His whole Word.*

How has understanding the passages about Joseph's extended family helped you understand Joseph's story better? Be specific.

3. Always take a God-centered approach.

Right application of Scripture is an outflow of right understanding of who God is.[8]

Have you ever heard the story of Joseph taught in a way that was not God-centered? How could you tell?

This story isn't meant to be extracted to stand alone, divorced from the rest of what God reveals in His Word. In telling the story of Joseph, God is telling a bigger story.

Review Romans 15:4. According to this verse, what are the stories of the patriarchs, like Joseph, supposed to give us?

We can't put our hope in Joseph. He's long gone. But we can put our hope in the One whose providence guided Joseph's life. As you keep reading Joseph's story, keep asking, "What does this reveal about God?"

The second key we've been given to understand the Bible is Jesus. He is our Rosetta Stone. Without Him, so much of Scripture simply wouldn't make sense. Part of being an effective student of the Word is training yourself to look for Jesus in the whole Bible, not just Matthew, Mark, Luke, and John. Erik Raymond writes,

> It's not just the big picture of Joseph's life that serves to underscore sovereignty. It's also the various components of his life. When we collect the details of Joseph's life we see a glorious reflection that closely mirrors another life we are so intimately familiar with. In fact, when you look at a list of the details, sometimes it's hard to discern whether we are talking about Joseph or Jesus. That is not because Joseph was Jesus' favorite Bible hero he wanted to emulate. It is because God is sovereign, and he has been laying the tracks for the glory of Christ throughout redemptive history.[9]

He then provides this list of similarities between Joseph and Jesus.

1. He is the object of his father's special love.
2. He had promises of divine exaltation.
3. He was mocked by his family.
4. He was sold for pieces of silver.

5. He was stripped of his robe.
6. He was delivered up to the Gentiles.
7. He was falsely accused.
8. He was faithful amid temptation.
9. He was thrown into prison.
10. He stood before rulers.
11. His power was acknowledged by those in authority.
12. He saves his rebellious brothers from death when they realize who he is.
13. He is exalted after and through humiliation.
14. He embraces God's purpose even though it brings him intense physical harm.
15. He is the instrument God uses at the hands of the Gentiles to bless his people.
16. He welcomes Gentiles to be part of his family.
17. He gives hungry people bread.
18. People must bow their knee before him.[10]

Circle the similarities on that list that you've never thought of before. Do you see additional similarities between Joseph and Jesus? Add them to the list.

To read the story of Joseph apart from the rest of Scripture is to miss the bigger, redemptive picture of God's generational work. And to study Joseph's story without looking for Jesus reduces it to an intellectual exercise more fitting for a history class than a Bible study.

TO READ THE STORY OF JOSEPH APART FROM THE REST OF SCRIPTURE IS TO MISS THE BIGGER, REDEMPTIVE PICTURE OF GOD'S GENERATIONAL WORK. AND TO STUDY JOSEPH'S STORY WITHOUT LOOKING FOR JESUS REDUCES IT TO AN INTELLECTUAL EXERCISE MORE FITTING FOR A HISTORY CLASS THAN A BIBLE STUDY.

Your love for the story of Joseph will expand exponentially when you look at it through the lens of the gospel.

How do you see God's bigger plan of redemption illustrated in the details of Joseph's life?

How does Joseph's character point forward to Jesus, the better Joseph?

These are not easy questions. There's no answer guide in the back of the Bible that can present them in simple terms. Yet, they are worth wrestling with, because they point us to the One that Joseph's life—*that your life*—is ultimately about.

Colossians 1:16–20 is a foundational passage for understanding Scripture and the world God made. Bottom line: It's all about Jesus.

Meditate on this passage by crossing out every "he" and "him" and replacing them with the name of Jesus. Then ask the Spirit to keep you Jesus-focused as you continue this study.

> **16** For by him all things were created, in heaven and on earth, visible and
> invisible, whether thrones or dominions or rulers or authorities—all things
> were created through him and for him. **17** And he is before all things, and in
> him all things hold together. **18** And he is the head of the body, the church.
> He is the beginning, the firstborn from the dead, that in everything he might
> be preeminent. **19** For in him all the fullness of God was pleased to dwell,
> **20** and through him to reconcile to himself all things, whether on earth or in
> heaven, making peace by the blood of his cross.

WEEK 4 | DAY 3

SNAPSHOT

Big idea: *Your family now is just a snapshot. You don't know what the album is going to look like yet.*

READ GENESIS 37:12–24

Rather than a life written into the pages of Scripture, try to imagine the story of Joseph as a series of photos on your phone.

His birth might be a snapshot of Rachel with tired eyes while gray-haired Jacob stood beaming beside her.

You could snap a pic of the day he received his coat of favor while the angry brothers scowled in the background.

Then another image of the brothers gathered around while Joseph gushed about the crazy dreams he'd been having.

Which brings us to another snapshot, a picture the brothers would hope no one would ever see.

Practice examining Scripture in context. According to Genesis 37:2, how old was Joseph at this time?

Joseph was old enough to tend the sheep with his brothers. That's what he was doing at the beginning of this chapter. But here, in verse 12, his brothers were pasturing sheep and Joseph got to stay home. Until Jacob sent the brother with whom the rest of the family could not even bear to speak to check on things.

What instructions did Jacob give Joseph in verse 14?

Based on what you already know about the relational dynamics of this family, why was this a doomed assignment?

Review Genesis 37:2. What kinds of stories did Joseph seem to like to tell about his brothers?

According to verse 18, when the brothers saw Joseph on the horizon, what did they decide to do?

That escalated quickly. Write down what each verse below records about the brothers' behavior:

Genesis 37:4

Genesis 37:8

Genesis 37:11

And then . . . by verse 18, Joseph's brothers saw that beautiful coat of his on the horizon and somebody said, "Let's kill him."

Read Genesis 37:18–24.

In the best of times, families remind each other what is true and spur each other on to live for God's glory. In the worst of times, families do the opposite, pulling each other away from God's best.

Enraged by bitter jealousy, what did the sons of Jacob do to their favored brother?

Read verse 25. What do you think this detail reveals about the condition of the brothers' hearts?

Can you imagine their callousness? As Joseph surely cried to be pulled from the pit . . .

"Guys, let me out of here."

"Guys, this isn't funny."

"Guys, I promise I won't tell Dad."

. . . his brothers sat down and ate their lunch.

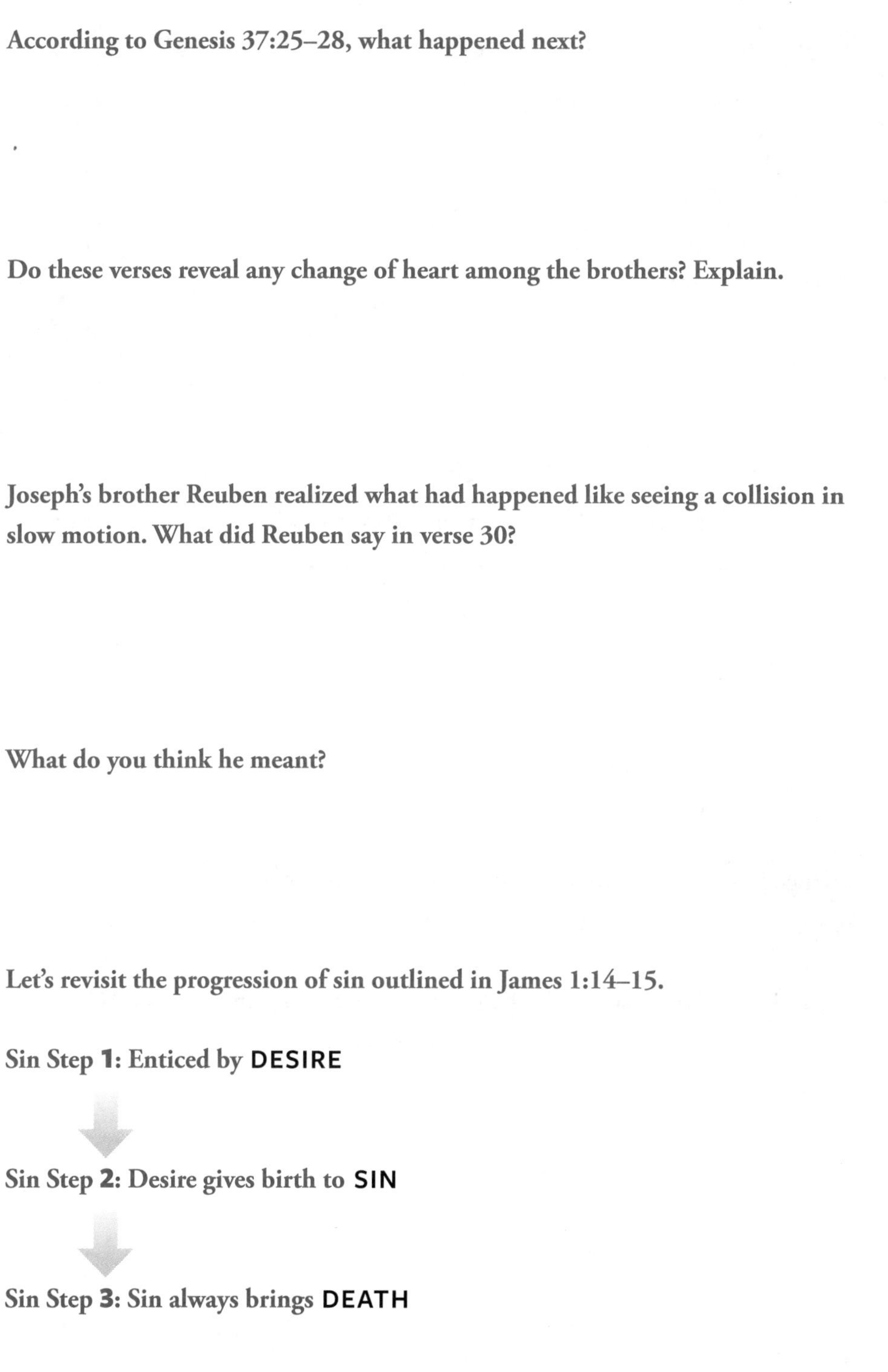

According to Genesis 37:25–28, what happened next?

Do these verses reveal any change of heart among the brothers? Explain.

Joseph's brother Reuben realized what had happened like seeing a collision in slow motion. What did Reuben say in verse 30?

What do you think he meant?

Let's revisit the progression of sin outlined in James 1:14–15.

Sin Step 1: Enticed by DESIRE

↓

Sin Step 2: Desire gives birth to SIN

↓

Sin Step 3: Sin always brings DEATH

What desires motivated Joseph's brothers to throw him into a pit?

What specific sin(s) did they commit?

Joseph didn't physically die in this moment. What other types of deaths did this family experience as a result of the brothers' sin?

Though the brothers tried to cover their tracks (more on that in the next week's study), there was no escaping the consequences of their choices.

What do you notice about Jacob's grief as recorded in verses 32–35? What were the relational implications of the brothers' sin?

We can't coat this moment in sugar. What happened in this family is ug-ly! Brother against brother in a murderous plot turned slave trade. Lies on top of lies. An already grieving father whose loss is so great he cannot be comforted. And a chosen son sent off to a foreign land to an uncertain future. Ah, but this is just a snapshot. The story of Joseph continues to teach us that *what God is doing now is not all that He is doing.*

It's true, God could have stopped Joseph from going to visit his brothers that day. He chose not to. He could have changed their hearts in an instant or sent an angelic warrior to guard the opening of the pit. He didn't. Instead of sending a rescue team, He sent foreign slave traders. What's up with that?

Joseph couldn't have seen it.

The brothers couldn't have seen it.

Jacob couldn't have seen it.

But God was at work. **God is always at work.**

One of my favorite thoughts on the ever-present providence of God comes from the Twitter thread of pastor John Piper: "God is always doing 10,000 things in your life, and you may be aware of three of them."[11]

If all we had was this moment in Joseph's family, we could only see pain, but it's just a snapshot. God was already moving this family toward redemption. The story of Joseph reminds us that when it comes to our families, we have a very finite, human perspective.

Let me take you through a mental photo album of my own family to show you what I mean:

- Jason and I broke up while we were dating. If you were just looking at a snapshot of that part of our lives, all you'd see were two kids who had no idea how to make a relationship work.

- We chose not to have kids for the first seven years of our marriage. If you were looking at that snapshot, you'd see two people more interested in having a career than a family.

- When I was twelve weeks pregnant with our first son, the doctor told us that he likely wouldn't make it, and we should abort him. If you took a snapshot of that moment, you'd see two very scared parents who had every reason to believe we'd never hold a baby of our own in our arms.

If you snapped a picture of us now, you'd see something that looks nearly the opposite of all those other photos. We've been happily married for more than twenty years. We made up for lost time and had four babies in ten years. And . . . I already told you about our Elisha. **To trust God with our families is to make peace with not being able to see the bigger picture.**

How does Job 26:14 describe what we see of God's ways?

God is not a lock to be picked, a code to be cracked, or a riddle to be solved. He's far too big for that! Which means we cannot always understand the ways He is at work in our families.

Perhaps when you think of your family, it feels like you're in the pit. You feel the sting of deep betrayal while it seems your family members are nonchalantly nibbling their lunch. Or you're experiencing Jacob-like grief. You can't be comforted. You can't imagine you will ever be comforted again. Maybe you're the older brother. Your sin has made such a mess of things, no cover up will suffice.

Again, the story of Joseph speaks. No matter how things look in this moment, this snapshot, God is at work. Rest assured, your limited perspective on what He is doing is far from the whole picture.

To wrap up today's study, doodle on Job 42:2. Write down names or circumstances where you need a fresh infusion of hope that God is at work in your family.

"I know that you can do all things,
and that no purpose of yours can be thwarted."
— Job 42:2

WEEK 4 | DAY 4

PLAY THE LONG GAME

Big idea: *God's timing is meant to sanctify you.*

READ 2 PETER 3:8–9

There is a door inside the Davis house that is sacred to me. It looks ordinary on the outside. If you open it, you'll just find the closet where our water heater is stored. You'll also find a story that God has been writing for many years.

The inside of that door is filled with hash marks. Beside each one is a name and a date where we have marked the height of our four sons. Day by day my boys look the same to me. They don't go to bed at night and wake up noticeably taller. But month by month, year by year, decade by decade, they are growing from tiny little babies who once fit inside my womb to grown men. (Please excuse me while I go have a little cry.)

This physical reality that children grow little by little—inch by inch—until they reach maturity is a beautiful picture of a spiritual reality of what God is doing in you, and in me.

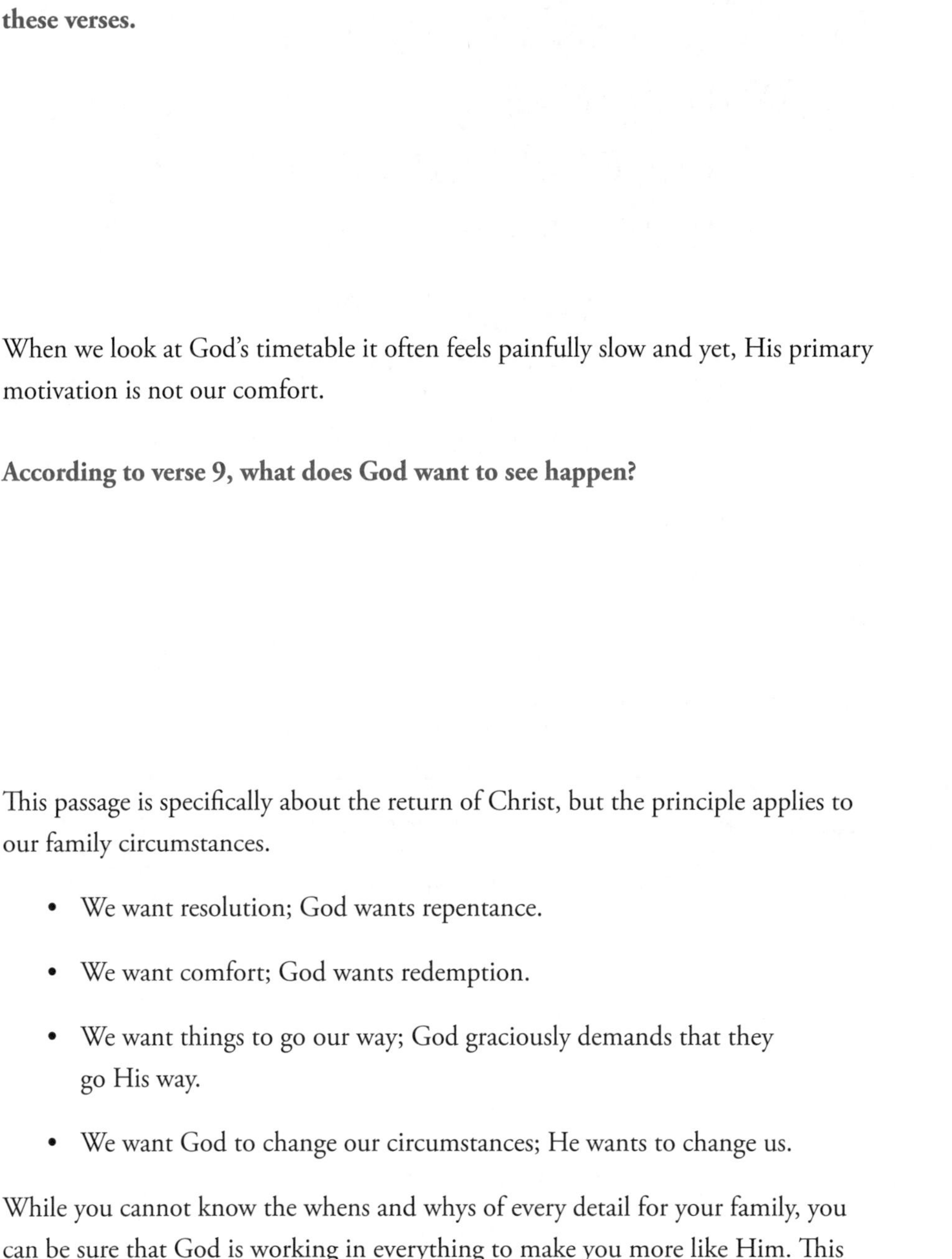

Review 2 Peter 3:8–9. Make a list of observations about God and time from these verses.

When we look at God's timetable it often feels painfully slow and yet, His primary motivation is not our comfort.

According to verse 9, what does God want to see happen?

This passage is specifically about the return of Christ, but the principle applies to our family circumstances.

- We want resolution; God wants repentance.
- We want comfort; God wants redemption.
- We want things to go our way; God graciously demands that they go His way.
- We want God to change our circumstances; He wants to change us.

While you cannot know the whens and whys of every detail for your family, you can be sure that God is working in everything to make you more like Him. This refining process is called sanctification.

WE WANT RESOLUTION;
GOD WANTS REPENTANCE.
WE WANT COMFORT;
GOD WANTS REDEMPTION.
WE WANT THINGS
TO GO OUR WAY;
GOD GRACIOUSLY DEMANDS
THAT THEY GO HIS WAY.
WE WANT GOD TO CHANGE
OUR CIRCUMSTANCES;
HE WANTS TO CHANGE US.

Write out your definition for sanctification below.

Sanctification is the process of progressively becoming more like Jesus, and I have great news: Sanctification is not something you achieve in your own strength. It is accomplished supernaturally by the Holy Spirit within you.

Read 2 Corinthians 3:18 below. Underline the way this verse describes how we are being transformed.

> And we all, with unveiled face, beholding the glory of the Lord, are being transformed into the same image from one degree of glory to another. For this comes from the Lord who is the Spirit.

You're not transforming yourself. God is using your family to transform you, right this very moment. We can't even change the smallest of habits without herculean effort and a high failure rate. By the power of the Holy Spirit, you are being transformed into the image of God "from one degree of glory to another."

Oh, I know the process seems painfully slow, but remember Peter's admonition, "The Lord is not slow to fulfill his promise as some count slowness, but is patient toward you" (v. 9).

One perspective Joseph's story gives us is that sometimes God works in decades, not days. Redemption takes a looooooong time in Joseph's family; perhaps it's because God not only works *for* us, He works *in* us. What a remarkable work He did in the hearts of Joseph's family members! What a remarkable work He is doing in you, *in your family.* Will you trust Him even if the process takes much longer than you'd like?

Wrap up today's study by making some notes beside the hash marks below.
How have you seen God work in your family already? Make a note.
How has He changed your heart toward a family member? Write it down.

#

#

#

#

For now, your spiritual progress may feel like nothing more than hash marks on the door, but you can trust that God is doing a more miraculous and transformational work in your family than you can ever imagine.

WEEK 4 | DAY 5

LEAVE A LEGACY OF PRAYER

You can have a profound influence on your family by developing the discipline of prayer. **Take time today to intercede for your family. Use the prompts below as a guide.**

Write down the names of the family members you want to pray for today. Next to each name, write down one need you want to see God meet.

Are there patterns of sin and brokenness that you need God to interrupt? Make a list and pray through it.

What can you praise God for about your family today?

What generational work do you want to see God do in your family? Write it out as a prayer.

Write out Philippians 4:7 as a prayer of blessing for your family.

Blessings & Curses

what:

Both the blessings of God and curses of sin will be passed from generation to generation.

so what?

God can use you to disrupt patterns of sin and bless the future generations of your family.

In 1874 a member of the New York State Prison Board noticed six members of one family were incarcerated at the same time. He started digging and traced the family line back to a man born in 1720 who was an alcoholic and notorious troublemaker who married a woman with similar sin patterns. They became the parents of eight children.

Of this couple's 1,200 descendants, born within the next 150 years:

- 310 were homeless
- 160 were prostitutes
- 180 suffered from drug or alcohol abuse
- 150 were criminals who spent time in prison, including seven for murder

The investigation also revealed that over the course of many years the state of New York had spent a fortune trying to rehabilitate the incarcerated members of this family, though none had made a significant, positive contribution to society.[12]

Exodus 34:7 records a bold paradigm:

> "I lavish unfailing love to a thousand generations.
> I forgive iniquity, rebellion, and sin.
> But I do not excuse the guilty.
> I lay the sins of the parents upon their children and grandchildren;
> the entire family is affected—
> even children in the third and fourth generations." (NLT)

As we continue studying the story of Joseph, we will see the effects of sin did, indeed, trickle down through the family line. More importantly, we will note that God can interrupt patterns of sin and wrong thinking and that His blessings last far beyond His judgment.

It's time for those favorite words of mine . . . **open your Bible** once more to Genesis 37.

WEEK 5 | DAY 1

THE LIES OUR FAMILIES TELL

Big idea: *Resist family secrets and embrace the rhythms of repentance, confession, and forgiveness.*

REVIEW GENESIS 37:18–35.

Do you notice any details you didn't see before? Jot down your notes below.

Two words have the power to wreak havoc on every family God's ever made: "Don't tell." Family secrets often begin as a single, cancerous cell, but they never stay contained. Soon enough those secrets metastasize and make us sick.

As we look again at this dark snapshot in Joseph's story, we see that Joseph's brothers saw that beautiful coat on the horizon and somebody whispered, "Let's kill him." Keep forcing yourself to peel back the layers. Keep reminding yourself that every text is part of a context.

What do we already know about the character of Simeon and Levi from Genesis 34:25–29?

While Genesis 37 records them herding sheep, these brothers were killers. They'd slaughtered all the men in the city where their sister's rapist lived. Scripture tells us that they plundered that city and took what they wanted, including human slaves (v. 29). One family secret tends to lead to more family secrets. How do I know what Simeon and Levi did was a secret?

What does Genesis 35:4 record?

These were some of the spoils of what the boys had stolen. Jacob didn't add them to the family treasury. He didn't sell them. *He buried them,* but some secrets are just too big to stay covered up:

> So when Joseph came to his brothers, they stripped him of his robe, the robe of many colors that he wore. (Gen. 37:23)

This step was about humiliation. The brothers forgot that all people are made in the image of God, a mistake that often has disastrous consequences in our own families. And then . . .

> And looking up they saw a caravan of Ishmaelites coming from Gilead, with their camels bearing gum, balm, and myrrh, on their way to carry it down to Egypt. (v. 25)

Underline what people group made up this caravan.

Ringing any mental bells? This is the joy of knowing our whole Bible. We get to see how the pieces interlock. Remember Joseph's family tree. Abraham had two sons with different women: Isaac and Ishmael. Ishmael was Joseph's grandpa's brother. Scripture is quite clear that Ishmael and his descendants would be men of war (Gen. 16:12). The brothers knew they were about to put Joseph in a terrible situation. They sold their hated brother to slave traders from the wrong side of the family. Now they had a secret, and secrets need kept.

Review Genesis 37:31–32. Write down the specific steps the brothers took to cover up their sin.

Notice the way they hedged their bets. This was deceit by omission.

My extended family has a way of talking about things sideways. We don't lie exactly . . . but we don't tell the whole truth either. It's a pattern I am praying the Lord will break with me. **Does your family have patterns related to truth and lies that He needs to break in you? Take a moment and ask the Lord, then write down what comes to mind.**

The brother's lie didn't buffer their dad from sorrow.

> Then Jacob tore his garments and put sackcloth on his loins and mourned for his son many days. All his sons and all his daughters rose up to comfort him, but he refused to be comforted and said, "No, I shall go down to Sheol to my son, mourning." Thus his father wept for him. (v. 34–35)

At any moment, somebody could have spoken up. Somebody could have said, "Dad, we made up the story. Joseph is alive. Let's go find him."

Based on your own family experiences, why do you think they didn't?

Does your family have secrets? I'm long enough in the tooth to know the answer is probably yes, though it might look a little different in each family:

- Sexual abuse
- Addiction
- Anger
- Infidelity . . .

No matter the flavor, secrets don't belong in the families of the people of God. **We're truth-telling people.**

Write out Proverbs 28:13 below.

This is a literary method often deployed in Scripture. **First, we're given something to avoid. Go back and underline that in the verse above. Then, following a "but," we're given a more excellent way. Circle it above.**

When it comes to sin, God asks for full disclosure. We can't hide anything from Him anyway. He sees what is done in secret (Matt. 6:4). There wasn't a single nanosecond that Joseph's brothers got away with their choice to enslave him. This also means that your family secrets, no matter how deeply buried, are fully exposed before the eyes of God.

Yet, how does God promise to respond to our sins when we bring them to Him in repentance according to James 5:16?

Many years ago, a mentor of mine taught me to pray that if there is sin in the lives of my husband and children that the Lord would expose it quickly. It's a prayer He has honored again and again.

As followers of Jesus, we can't bury our sin under a tree. We shouldn't seek to cover it up. We must drag it into the light and build families where the essential rhythms of repentance, confession, and forgiveness are normal and expected.

Wrap up today's study by writing out a heartfelt prayer, confessing any family secrets or sins you've attempted to hide and asking the Lord to expose sin in others so that your family can live in greater freedom.

WEEK 5 | DAY 2

REUBEN'S REGRET

Big Idea: *You can surrender your regrets to God, trusting Him to work all things to your good and His glory.*

READ GENESIS 30:14–18.

When you think about your family, do you have any regrets? Start a list below.

Read Genesis 37:18–24 again. This time, pay attention to Reuben. In the space below, note any observations you make about his character.

According to Genesis 29:31–32, where did Reuben fit in the line-up of Joseph's brothers?

Reuben was the first of Jacob's twelve sons. Like many firstborns, he was highly responsible, a good boy who wanted to please his momma. How do I know? Buckle up—we're about to work through a weird story. Let me set the stage with Genesis 30:1:

> When Rachel saw that she bore Jacob no children, she envied her sister. She said to Jacob, "Give me children, or I shall die!"

The rest of the chapter records the sisters shoving their servants toward Jacob trying to win the battle of fertility. Jacob obliged, so there was a lot of sex happening and a lot of babies being born who shared the same dad (Jacob) but had different mommas.

Read Genesis 30:14–18. What did Reuben find in the field?

Who did he give them to?

Why do you think Rachel wanted the mandrakes so badly?

It's okay if you need to brush up on your ancient Middle Eastern horticulture. Mandrakes are perennial herbs that grow in sandy soil like the land where Jacob raised his family. Their roots look remarkably like a human body.[13] Likely because of this, mandrakes have long been used in "love potions" and thought to boost fertility.[14]

Keep training yourself to see every text within context. Rachel and Leah were locked in a battle to see who could have more of Jacob's babies. Perhaps Reuben saw his mom's distress and just wanted to make her happy, so he brought her something that might help.

Review Genesis 30:16. What words would you use to describe Leah's tone with her husband?

This was a marriage built on manipulation. Remember that Leah was not the loved wife. Desperate to turn her husband's affections toward her, she hired him for his sexual availability with a crop of roots and berries brought to her by her oldest boy.

Now is a good time to repeat an important theme: all families are broken by sin. **This means all families are an opportunity for God to bring redemption.**

Leah didn't need the mandrakes. She and Jacob conceived another son that night. Leah named him Issachar which means "wages" or "hire." *Ick.*

Genesis 30 shows Reuben as a son who desired to please his momma, but he was far from a perfect boy.

What event does Genesis 35:22 record?

So much of our brokenness rears its ugly head in our families in the form of sexual dysfunction. A son sleeping with his father's concubine certainly qualifies.

Let's head back to Genesis 37. **Read Reuben's words again in verses 21–22. Based on what you've learned about Reuben's character, why do you think he acted this way?**

Reuben had sinned against his father once. Here, it seems, he decided he would not do it again. He did suggest the pit, but pay attention to his motive.

What was Reuben's intention (v. 22)?

Instead of standing up for what was right, instead of stepping into his role as the oldest—a leader among the brothers—Reuben took a passive aggressive approach.

Are there any specific fears that make it difficult for you to stand up for what's right in your family?

We don't know where Reuben went for verses 25–28. That's the part of the story where the brothers ate lunch near the pit they'd hurled Joseph into; but in verse 29, Reuben came back, presumably to set things right.

Read Genesis 37:29–30 one more time. What emotions do you hear under Reuben's words? Make a list.

Imagine Reuben's inner struggle . . .

- as the brothers tore Joseph's robe.
- as they walked back home.
- as they lied to their father.
- as he watched his dad double over with grief.

How many times did he replay the events that led to his brother's exile in his mind? How many times did he wish he'd said something different? The Bible doesn't say this, but human experience convinces me that Reuben had regrets as deep as the pit his brother was thrown into. Maybe you do too.

Romans 8:28 is an anchor we are wise to tether our families to. Write it out below.

God has graciously made a way for us to experience forgiveness for our sins and shortcomings, but He has not erased them. The way we treat each other matters. But He is using it—*all of it*—for our good and His glory.

Your best day as a mom? God is using that.
Your worst day as a mom? God is using that.
The happiest day of your marriage? God is using that.
The day you did something that could have caused your marriage to end? God is using that.
The things you said to your parents in anger? God is using that.
The time you weren't there for your sister? God is using that.

To live out God's Word is to take our regrets and to lay them at the foot of the cross and trust that God can redeem even *this.*

Revisit Romans 8. This time, run it back a few verses. According to verse 26 what is it the Spirit's job to help us with?

Reuben had regrets. As Joseph's story unfolds, we will see that God used them. *He uses it all.*

Revisit your list of regrets at the top of this session. Add any more the Spirit has brought to mind as you've studied today. Then take a red marker and write boldly across the entire list: *God uses it all.*

He does, you know? Rest in that today.

WEEK 5 | DAY 3

FAMINE & FAVOR

Big idea: *God dramatically orchestrated unlikely circumstances and brought Joseph's family back together.*

READ GENESIS 42–43

As we pick up Joseph's story, he's not a teenager anymore. For the purposes of this study, we're going to skip Genesis 38 through most of 41. Not because those verses don't matter. Of course they do, they are as inspired by the Holy Spirit as the rest of Scripture and they include some fascinating twists and turns, including the scandalous story of Tamar and one of Joseph's brothers, Judah. Because I want you to know and love your whole Bible, I'd encourage you to read those chapters on your own. The bottom line of those pages is more sexual dysfunction. These chapters also describe Joseph in Potiphar's house and an incident that got Joseph thrown into another pit, this time, a prison (Gen. 39:19–23).

Though we won't dive deep into these chapters here, one theme is too important to miss.

Read Genesis 39:21. Remember our primary question: What do you learn about God in this single verse?

It's tempting to respond to verses like this with Sunday school answers, but think about all you've learned.

Joseph's mom was dead.
His brothers hated his guts.
He'd been sold to slave traders for a little bit of silver.
He was forcibly removed from his homeland and taken into foreign territory.
He was a servant in the house of a powerful man.

And yet . . . Scripture says Joseph was loved steadfastly and given God's favor. How can this be true?

No amount of dysfunction in Joseph's family could change God's affection and attention toward him, nor do the pain points in your family disrupt His love and care for you.

Chapter 40 records Joseph interpreting the dreams of two fellow prisoners. In chapter 41, after two long years in prison, the highest ruler of Egypt started having disturbing nightmares. Once again, Joseph was pulled from the pit. The chapter ends with Joseph, the shepherd, turned slave, turned prisoner . . . the dreamer turned interpreter, giving instructions to Pharoah.

Read Genesis 41:34–36 below. Underline all of the verbs. Circle why Joseph encouraged Pharoah to take these steps.

> **34** "Let Pharaoh proceed to appoint overseers over the land and take one-fifth
> of the produce of the land of Egypt during the seven plentiful years. **35** And
> let them gather all the food of these good years that are coming and store up grain under the authority of Pharaoh for food in the cities, and let them keep it. **36** That food shall be a reserve for the land against the seven years of famine that are to occur in the land of Egypt, so that the land may not perish through the famine."

Seeing Joseph's wisdom, Pharaoh appointed him to a position of power.

According to Genesis 41:41, what territory became Joseph's to rule?

Not only did Joseph's status change, but his family also changed. Match the following verses with the family event recorded.

Genesis 41:46	Joseph became a father
Genesis 41:45	Joseph turned 30
Genesis 41:50	Joseph got married

Read Genesis 41:51–52. Write down the names of Joseph's sons and what each name meant. What do these names reveal about what was going on in Joseph's heart?

Joseph settled down, started a family, and got busy preparing Egypt for the coming famine. Just as he predicted, Egypt experienced seven years of plenty (Gen. 41:53) before the seven years of famine began. There's nothing quite like hard times to bring a family together.

What does Genesis 41:56–57 reveal about the scope of the famine?

Imagine if Joseph's brothers hadn't sent him away to another land. Could he have used his gifts to protect them from the famine? We'll never know.

Read Genesis 42:1–5. Make a list of observations.

Only God could orchestrate this! These brothers had sinned: against their dad, against their brother, and most importantly against God. Thirteen years had passed, but time doesn't heal all wounds. I'm sure each brother handled the guilt a little differently. Some probably put the act out of their minds completely; some likely shifted the blame; perhaps a few worried constantly that they'd be found out. But while the eleven sons of Jacob were back home with a father changed by grief, God was caring for the cast-aside brother. He was making a way for the wrong to be made right.

A question I need to keep asking is: *Do you trust that God is at work in the dysfunctional places of your family?* It probably won't happen on your schedule. It likely won't look like you think it should. I doubt Joseph and his brothers could have imagined what was about to unfold, but God was at work. *God is at work.* Scripture tells us He is making all things new (Rev. 21:5). If there's a part of your family where you've lost hope, the next chapter of the story of Joseph is for you.

To wrap up today's study, write out a prayer honestly expressing areas of your family's story where you've lost hope. Ask the Lord to give you faith that He is doing more than you can imagine.

WEEK 5 | DAY 4

THE SINS OF THE FATHER

Big Idea: *Sin has a generational impact on our families. So does God's grace.*

READ GENESIS 42; EXODUS 34:6–7

While Joseph's story beautifully illustrates the generational blessings of God, it also highlights a darker reality: Sin has a terrible trickle-down effect. Your life is profoundly impacted by the rebellion of your foreparents and future generations will be shaped by the many ways you miss the mark.

Read Genesis 42:6–11. What were the dreams referenced in verse 9? Write down what you remember. (Hint: sheaves and stars.)

Read Genesis 42:9–11. Did Joseph's brothers tell the truth?

Yes, they were brothers, but I wouldn't call them honest. Remember, they let their dad believe that Joseph was dead, torn apart by wild animals. Despite his deep and obvious grief, they chose to keep what they'd done a secret for thirteen years. Deception was a character flaw they came by honestly.

Look up Genesis 25:26. Does your Bible include a footnote with an explanation of the meaning of Jacob's name? If so, write down what it says.

Most translations make a note on this verse that Jacob's name means "heel grabber" or "cheater." Some scholars translate his name as "deceiver."[15] Jacob's story fleshes this out. Jacob manipulated, connived, and cheated many of his family members. He was known to do whatever it took to get what he wanted. The old adage is true; the apple rarely falls far from the tree.

This little verse that records deceitful, jealous men lying about whether or not they were liars reminds me of something the Bible proclaims about every family.

Let's jump ahead to Exodus 20:4–6. Every text is part of a context, and the context here is the Ten Commandments. Read these verses and look for family language.

4 "You shall not make for yourself a carved image, or any likeness of anything
that is in heaven above, or that is in the earth beneath, or that is in the water
under the earth. 5 You shall not bow down to them or serve them, for I the
Lord your God am a jealous God, visiting the iniquity of the fathers on the
children to the third and the fourth generation of those who hate me,
6 but showing steadfast love to thousands of those who love me and keep my
commandments."

Underline verse 5. What does this verse reveal about the consequences of sin? Be specific.

Ezekiel 18:19–20 offers a counter perspective. Write out these verses below.

Which is it? Are the sins of the father (or mother) passed to future generations or are the consequences of sin contained to the offender? To answer that question, it's essential to know the character of God, which we learn through His Word. Because God is perfectly just, this idea of sins being passed is not punitive. It's not a punishment. Rather, the Bible is describing an undeniable reality. **Our sin impacts those who we live closest to.**

Here's a new Scrabble word for you: epigenetics. This is "the study of heritable changes in gene function that do not involve changes in DNA sequence."[16]

Rewrite that definition in your own words.

I'd say it this way: Epigenetics is the study of how changes in our genetic make-up can be passed down. It's a developing science, but experts now say that trauma, which is often a result or a showcase of our brokenness, can be passed through our genes up to four generations.[17] To which God's Word proclaims, "Yeah! I've been telling you that for a long time!"

Circle back to Exodus 20:5. How many generations does the Bible say the iniquity of parents will be passed?

Don't you love it when science catches up to the inspired Word of God?!

A cultural conversation of our day is whether or not people are born with a bent toward things that the Bible defines as sin. We already know the commonsense answer to this question.

- Angry parents raise angry children.
- The abused often become abusers.
- Children from divorced homes, like me, are more likely to get divorced.[18]
- Addicts often raise addicts.

And as we see in the story of Joseph . . . sometimes liars raise liars. It makes me think about the times in my life when I've needed to clean out the house of a family member who died. I remember looking around at all the stuff my grandparents or aunts and uncles collected and thinking, "It's junk! I don't want this stuff."

All of us, to one degree or another, can look around at the sin patterns of our family and say, "This is junk! I don't want this stuff." And yet, sometimes it feels inescapable. Do we look at Joseph's family and say, "They couldn't help it. Their dad was a liar. They were liars. They probably raised children who were liars"? Not if we read our whole Bible.

Go back to Exodus 20:4–6. What beautiful promise does God make in verse 6?

How have you seen this promise fulfilled in your own family?

It's true that our sin can have a lasting impact on our families, even after we're gone. But that's not the last word. *Every* story of how the effects of sin are passed among the generations can be punctuated by this good news: "But God!" His intention is to bless us, generation to generation to generation, up to a thousand generations, if that's how long it takes Him to come back. Not a word in the Word is wasted. The numbers listed in these verses are not accidental.

How many generations are listed for the impact of sin (v. 5)?

How many generations are listed for the blessings of obedience (v. 6)?

God's grace lasts infinitely longer than His wrath!

Yes, patterns of sin often get repeated, but the Bible tells this story too:

- God turned families of fishermen into fishers of men.
- He transformed prostitutes into proclaimers of truth.
- He replaced generational poverty with spiritual riches.

God used Joseph's life to interrupt the pattern of his family. It's not too late for God to interrupt the cycles of sin in your family too.

Slowly read through Exodus 34:6–7 below. Underline how God describes Himself.

> **6** The Lord passed before him and proclaimed, "The Lord, the Lord, a God
> merciful and gracious, slow to anger, and abounding in steadfast love and
> faithfulness, 7 keeping steadfast love for thousands, forgiving iniquity and
> transgression and sin, but who will by no means clear the guilty, visiting the
> iniquity of the fathers on the children and the children's children, to the third
> and the fourth generation."

God is a generational God. He is also merciful and gracious, slow to anger, and abounding in steadfast love for you and *every* generation of your family.

What are the patterns of sin and wrong thinking in your family you want God to stop? Make a list and then ask God to make you like Joseph, a disruptor of multigenerational iniquity and a conduit of blessing for the descendants to come.

WEEK 5 | DAY 5

LEAVE A LEGACY OF PRAYER

You can have a profound influence on your family by developing the discipline of prayer. **Take time today to intercede for your family. Use the prompts below as a guide.**

Write down the names of the family members you want to pray for today. Next to each name, write down one need you want to see God meet.

Are there patterns of sin and brokenness that you need God to interrupt? Make a list and pray through it.

What can you praise God for about your family today?

What generational work do you want to see God do in your family? Write it out as a prayer.

Write out Ephesians 3:16 as a prayer of blessing for your family.

Reunions, Reconciliation & Redemption

what:

There is a bedrock truth that transforms the way we operate within our families: God has a plan.

so what?

You can relinquish the illusion of control and surrender your family to God.

Like a balloon inflated beyond capacity, we've come to a point in Joseph's story filled with tension. The pin that will pop it is providence.

Nearly two decades have passed since Joseph was sold and a lie wrapped itself tightly around his family. Surely, many of those years were filled with humdrum family life. Sheep needed to be

WEEK 6

sheared. Dinner needed to be made. Secrets needed to be kept. Ah, but that can only ever be the lower story. The higher story is what God was up to. He is *always* moving things along by His goodness and mercy.

This week of study will require heart work on your part. You'll need to "trust fall" into your own understanding and acceptance of God's plan. You'll invite the Spirit to test the hardness of your heart. You'll see your own family tree in black and white, including the branches you wish were different. There may be uncomfortable moments, but each one will move you toward this profound truth uttered by our boy, Joseph: "God sent me before you to preserve for you a remnant on earth, and to keep alive for you many survivors. *So it was not you who sent me here, but God*" (Gen. 45:7–8).

It's time to **open your Bible** again. We'll start in Genesis 42.

WEEK 6 | DAY 1

A RECKONING

Big Idea: *The plans of man cannot stop the plans of God.*

READ GENESIS 42

Before you jump back into the story of Joseph, spend a few moments meditating on Job 42:2. You can doodle thoughts and images in the space below.

"I know that you can do all things,
and that no purpose of yours can be thwarted."
— Job 42:2

Those words were spoken by Job, a man who suffered the loss of his fortune, his family, and his sure footing in the world. Ultimately Job concluded that God's providence could not be thwarted by his pain. I like to use my sanctified imagination to picture Job and Joseph comparing notes in heaven. Both men suffered greatly. Both were misunderstood and mistreated, and both experienced the mystery Job uttered. Perhaps they'd lean back in their chairs and happily sigh: "Truly God can do *all* things. No purpose of His can ever be thwarted." You'll see this dramatically illustrated in Joseph's story today.

Summarize the highlights from Genesis 42:1–17 below.

-
-
-
-
-
-

Review Genesis 42:18–22. How did Reuben describe what was happening? (v. 22)

What emotions do you recognize beneath Reuben's words?

Reuben, it seems, had carried his regret all these years. Joseph's cries from the pit haunted him; and now, when trouble came, he was sure it was penance for his sin.

How does Genesis 42:24 describe Joseph's reaction to his brother's words?

What emotions do you recognize beneath Joseph's tears?

Joseph's heart was stirred by his brother's confession, but he also took Simeon (you might remember him as the brother who helped kill a village of men) and told the remaining brothers that they could have him back only if they brought Benjamin to Egypt.

What was unique about Joseph and Benjamin's relationship within the family? (See Gen. 35:24.)

As the brothers prepared to return to their father with grain and grim news, Joseph secretly replaced the money they'd paid to purchase it.

Review Genesis 42:26–28. When they discovered the money had been returned to their sack, who did they blame? (v. 28)

Does this reveal a change of heart in the brothers? Explain.

When Jacob heard the news that Simeon had been taken captive and that he would only be released if Benjamin was brought to Egypt, he did not take it well.

According to Genesis 42:38, what was his first response?

Eventually Jacob relented. Write Jacob's words recorded in Genesis 43:13–14.

Based on his reaction, where do you think Jacob ultimately put his hope? Explain your answer.

Jacob had tried to mitigate risk by keeping Benjamin at home. When that didn't work, he had a difficult choice to make. He could refuse to let Benjamin out of his sight, knowing that his older son, Simeon, would stay incarcerated and his family might starve to death; or he could take his hands off the proverbial wheel and trust that his sons were in the hand of God.

What attribute of God did Jacob seem to focus on? (v. 14)

What do you think Jacob meant when he said, "As for me, if I am bereaved of my children, I am bereaved"? Do you think he had given up hope?

Imagine how differently Jacob would have written the story of his family.

When his wife faced a difficult delivery of their son Benjamin, what outcome would Jacob have likely chosen?

When his son Joseph began having strange dreams, what outcome would Jacob have likely chosen?

When his sons' anger and resentment toward one another turned into hatred, what outcome would Jacob have likely chosen?

When he sent Joseph to check on his brothers in the field, what outcome would Jacob have likely chosen?

When famine began to encroach on the borders of his family's land, what outcome would Jacob have likely chosen?

When he sent his sons to buy grain in Egypt, what outcome would Jacob have likely chosen?

One way to view the story of Joseph is that nothing went Jacob's (or Joseph's) way. But there is another lens, a better way to view every story. Providence is the perspective that shows us that *everything went God's way*. Certainly, we don't always walk the perfect path God would choose for His children, for God never wants us to experience sin or the devastation of it, but no parts of this story ever spun out of His control. **No parts of your story ever spin out of His control.** The plans of man can never stop the plans of God.

The application of the text is as obvious as it is challenging: We can surrender our families to God knowing that His plans will ultimately be accomplished, or we can continue to live white-knuckled, desperately clinging to the way we want things to go. Either way, Job's words are true: No plan of God's can be thwarted.

To wrap up today's study, make a list of things that aren't going the way you want them to. Be honest with yourself and with God. Then follow Jacob's lead. Write down the attributes of God you can put your hope in today as an expression of surrender to His will and ways.

WEEK 6 | DAY 2

TWO PATHS DIVERGE

Big Idea: *Resist hard-heartedness. Stay soft.*

READ GENESIS 43

There is a thick, blue book that sits near my desk, a gift given to me by my husband several Christmases ago. It is a collection of works from my favorite poet, Robert Frost. The binding falls open easily to page 105 because I've read the words of "The Road Not Taken" so often. I bet you know these familiar lines:

> Two roads diverged in a yellow wood,
> And sorry I could not travel both
> And be one traveler, long I stood.[19]

Many literary professors have asked their students to defend what the two paths are. Let's just say that for our purposes the two paths are hard-heartedness and soft-heartedness. The path you choose will make a significant difference in the temperature and tone of your family.

Genesis 43 finds the brothers desperate again. They had to saddle their donkeys and head back to Egypt, this time with brother Benjamin in tow.

Review Genesis 43:16–33. Write down your observations about how the brothers treated each other in this interaction.

Observations About How Joseph Treated His Brothers	Observations About How the Brothers Treated Joseph

Joseph held all the cards. He had enough power to imprison all his brothers. He could have thrown them into a pit to see how they liked it or sold them as slaves to be carted off to another land. Humanly speaking, he had every right to choose revenge or punishment in the face of such profound rejection and mistreatment. Joseph could have hardened his heart toward his brothers.

Or . . .

He could choose the other way, the second path. It's a way we can only embrace with the help of the Holy Spirit living within us, the way we *must* take to build God-honoring families.

See if you can spot it in Genesis 43:29–30. Underline Joseph's response to his brothers.

> **29** And he lifted up his eyes and saw his brother Benjamin, his mother's son, and said, "Is this your youngest brother, of whom you spoke to me? God be gracious to you, my son!" **30** Then Joseph hurried out, for his compassion grew warm for his brother, and he sought a place to weep. And he entered his chamber and wept there.

After all these years and so much pain, Joseph still had a soft spot in his heart for his brother. This is the second time the Bible records Joseph weeping for his brothers: The first was for the brothers who sinned against him (Gen. 42:24), and this time for the only other son of Rachel.

Joseph models an important reality for us here: God's people are to be soft-hearted people.

Write out Ezekiel 11:19 and Ezekiel 36:26 in the chart below. Draw a heart around the word heart every time it appears.

Ezekiel 11:19	Ezekiel 36:26

There's a beautiful parallel happening here. You can only see it if you know your whole Bible. In Exodus God gave the law to Moses. He carved it on tablets of stone (Ex. 31:18). Part of what Jesus did was establish a new covenant, not on tablets of stone, but written on our hearts. In Hebrews 10:16, the Holy Spirit declares,

> "This is the covenant that I will make with them
>   after those days, declares the Lord:
> I will put my laws on their hearts,
>   and write them on their minds."

He gives us this word picture to help us understand how the gospel transforms us. We don't have hearts hardened by sin anymore. God has mercifully given us soft hearts of flesh. Consider these parallels from the Word.

Hard hearts ignore the needs of others. (Deut. 15:7–8)
Soft hearts resist compassion fatigue and keep caring. (Eph. 4:32)

Hard hearts turn a blind eye to the sick and disabled. (Mark 3:5)
Soft hearts are moved by the suffering of others. (Matt. 25:40)

Hard hearts justify sin and refuse to repent. (2 Chron. 36:13)
Soft hearts are broken by sin and repent often. (Joel 2:13)

Hard hearts withhold forgiveness. (Matt. 18:22–35)
Soft hearts forgive freely, acutely aware that they've been freely forgiven. (Col. 3:13)

Hard hearts are unchanged by the Word. (Zech. 7:12)
Soft hearts feel a desperate dependence on the Word. (Ps. 119)

Hard hearts cheapen grace by persisting in known sin. (Rom. 2:4–5)

Soft hearts are brokenhearted by sin and desperate for the Spirit's help to pursue holiness. (Rom. 8:12–13)

Hard hearts obsess over the failures and shortcomings of others. (Matt. 7:3–5)
Soft hearts recognize their own weakness and focus their prayers on "Lord, change me!" (Rom. 12:3)

Hard hearts need to be right. (Prov. 12:15)
Soft hearts long to be righteous. (Phil. 3:9)

Hard hearts grumble. They are never satisfied. (Ex. 16:8)
Soft hearts are grateful, recognizing the elaborate gifts God has already given. (Col. 3:15)

Hard hearts isolate, telling themselves that others would come to them if they really cared. (Prov. 18:1)
Soft hearts depend on other believers for accountability, correction, wisdom, and friendship. (Prov. 13:20)[20]

Based on this list, do you have a hard heart or a soft heart?

Joseph was a sinner in need of grace just like his brothers. The gospel radically transforms the way we operate within our families because it reminds us that every single member of our family is a sinner in need of a savior.

Family life provides a million reasons to become hard-hearted. We all experience frequent misunderstandings, words that hurt, and unmet expectations. Sometimes there are betrayals. Sometimes there is abuse.

As Joseph faced those who had inflicted so much harm, he did not harden his heart. He wept for his brothers. His heart was warm toward them and filled with genuine compassion. He chose the better path: the path of forgiveness, of humility, of grace toward undeserving sinners.

A life of tenderness toward your family will not be easy. Seeing your family members with compassion will go against every inclination of your flesh. Forgiveness can feel so much harder than holding on to hurt. But Robert Frost got it right.

> I shall be telling this with a sigh
> Somewhere ages and ages hence:
> Two roads diverged in a wood, and I—
> I took the one less traveled by,
> And that has made all the difference.[21]

What command does Psalm 95:8 give?

Put this into practice by praying through the hard-hearted vs. soft-hearted list above. Make note of any areas where your heart has grown hard toward your family and ask God to soften you.

WEEK 6 | DAY 3

LIVES TIED TOGETHER

Big Idea: *Stay tethered to your family.*

READ GENESIS 44

As you've worked through this study, have you wondered about the specifics of my family? I've certainly wondered about yours. It wouldn't be loving for me to put everything my family faces in a Bible study for the masses, but I can let you in on some of the highlights (or lowlights, as the case may be).

- I'm from a divorced home. My parents split when I was ten, a decision that still sends shock waves into the way I see and operate within my family 30+ years later.
- I'm estranged from my dad. We haven't spoken in years.
- My mom is terminally ill. We've watched her suffer for a long time now.
- My relationship with some of my siblings is strained at best. Though our life experiences are similar, we struggle to see them the same way.
- We've had an unusual amount of grief in recent years. We've planned *a lot* of funerals.

I'm not trying to win some twisted bragging contest. I don't believe my family is unusual or particularly painful. We're just sinners trying to live with other sinners. Since that rarely goes perfectly, I know what it's like to wish that things were different, but the story of Joseph is teaching me to lean into, rather than resist, the ties that bind.

We've been systematically studying the life of Joseph, and we've found plenty of evidence of dysfunction: brother against brother, sister against sister, wife against husband . . . deceit, violence, abandonment, grief. All of this, and more, is hanging from the branches of Joseph's family tree.

We left off in Genesis 43 with Joseph and his brothers back together. There had been a reckoning, but not reconciliation . . . not yet.

I don't want to skip Genesis 44. There's gold in them thar hills! Actually, it was silver.

What did Joseph command in Genesis 44:1–2?

What happened next according to Genesis 44:3–5?

Why do you think Joseph did this? Base your answer on what you've learned about his character.

Review Genesis 44:6–13 below. Underline the words of Joseph's steward. Circle the brothers' words. Put a star beside the name of the brother the silver cup was found in.

> **6** When he overtook them, he spoke to them these words. **7** They said to him,
> "Why does my lord speak such words as these? Far be it from your servants
> to do such a thing! **8** Behold, the money that we found in the mouths of our
> sacks we brought back to you from the land of Canaan. How then could we
> steal silver or gold from your lord's house? **9** Whichever of your servants is
> found with it shall die, and we also will be my lord's servants." **10** He said,
> "Let it be as you say: he who is found with it shall be my servant, and the
> rest of you shall be innocent." **11** Then each man quickly lowered his sack to
> the ground, and each man opened his sack. **12** And he searched, beginning
> with the eldest and ending with the youngest. And the cup was found in
> Benjamin's sack. **13** Then they tore their clothes, and every man loaded his
> donkey, and they returned to the city.

Can't you just picture them? All lined up in a row; oldest to youngest. First, Reuben, then Simeon, Levi, Judah, Dan, Naphtali, Gad, Asher, Issachar, Zebulun, and finally, Benjamin. The cup was found in Baby Brother's sack, the boy they'd promised their bereaved father they'd bring back unharmed.

Read Judah's words found in Genesis 44:14–18. What reason did Judah give for why they now faced this hardship? (v. 16)

Do you think he was right?

What happened next according to Genesis 44:14?

Bells should be ringing in that beautiful brain of yours. Remember the dreams that started this family feud?

Just for kicks, revisit Genesis 37:5–11, and summarize the dreams below.

And what did the brothers say in Genesis 37:8?

They would. *They did.* As the brothers bowed, Judah begged.

Read Judah's passionate speech from Genesis 44:18–34. Write down your observations below.

How did Judah describe the connection between Jacob and Benjamin in verse 30? What do you think he meant?

You've heard the phrase "the ties that bind"? It's an idiom that describes the invisible chords that link us together. Throughout human history, the strength and power of family bonds have been an obvious, inescapable reality. We live in an era with a new twist. Don't like your family? Get a new one. Hit a rough patch? Abandon ship. If God's design for the family unit doesn't match what you want, build a new kind of family. Carefully select a group of friends who look like you, think like you, and adore you and make them your family. Except, family is God's idea, and the family you're in was chosen for you by a God who loves you.

Even as I type these words, I can feel some resistance. Every image bearer of God has the right to get themselves to safety if a family situation becomes dangerous and not every family member is a wise choice to spend lots of time with. I get that. *I live that*, but family is not a concept we can interchange with friend or coworker. Like Jacob and Benjamin, our lives are bound up in the lives of those on our family tree.

Part of the reason I started this lesson with some insights into my family is to show that I know how challenging this can be. Do I wish God had given me a dad who stayed? I do. Do I wish He hadn't chosen to allow my mom to get sick with a terrible terminal disease? Of course! Do I wish all members of my family always got along perfectly? Desperately. I've also seen His hand in all of it. He's used the good and the bad, the highs and the lows, the wins and the heartaches to show me who He is. This is one of the most powerful lessons God can use the story of Joseph to teach us.

Would Joseph's life have been easier with different brothers? Maybe. But easy isn't God's goal. He chose Joseph's family to accomplish His purposes, just like He's chosen yours.

Does this perspective shift anything in your heart? If so, in what way?

You've visualized Joseph's family tree. Now, it's time to do your own. Use the graphic below to illustrate the family God has given you, not the family you wish you had. Not every branch will be straight and fruitful, but none of them will be accidental. Before you start, pray this prayer.

Lord, thank You for creating the family. Thank You for creating my family. Teach me to embrace it rather than resisting it. Help me see the ways You use my family to make me more like You. Amen.

WEEK 6 | DAY 4

GOD SENT ME BEFORE YOU

Big Idea: *There is nothing God can't redeem.*

READ GENESIS 45; COLOSSIANS 1:11–14

As we turn the page to Genesis 45, once again we find Joseph overcome with emotion. To help put yourself in Joseph's shoes, write down a summary of his interactions with his brothers from the past three chapters of Genesis.

-
-
-
-

What did Joseph do according to Genesis 45:2?

Have you ever had a cry like that? A heaving, full-body cry? Try to picture yourself in that emotional state, then read what happened next.

What bold words did Joseph finally say in verse 3? Write them down.

Let's keep reading. This is getting good! Write down Joseph's words from verses 4–7.

According to verse 8, who did Joseph think sent him to Egypt?

There it is, the bedrock truth that transforms the way we see our families and operate within them: **God has a plan.** This is a radical worldview! Joseph had been forcibly taken from his homeland, ripped from the arms of the father who loved him, enslaved and imprisoned. Yet, he did not blame God. He believed, rightly, that God allowed the whole thing.

How could embracing this perspective change the way you see your own family?

We could have taken a thousand snapshots of Joseph's family, put them in an album, and it would have seemed like nothing good could ever come from this fractured and flawed family.

Think back to the family tree when Sarah was old and barren. Snap a picture. *What can God do with that?*

Remember when Jacob and Esau were so angry at each other that Esau planned to kill his twin. *What can God do with that?*

Think about the two sisters who were forced to live within a polygamist marriage built on deep hurt and profound dysfunction. *What can God do with that?*

Remember that one of the daughters of that union was raped. *What can God do with that?* Or when her brothers repaid evil with more evil. *What can God do with that?*

Consider that Joseph's brothers sold their own flesh and blood into slavery and then covered it up for years. *What can God do with that?*

Have you met this God?! How does Psalm 100:5 describe Him?

What sets Joseph apart was not that his family had dysfunction, but that he seemed to trust, *really trust,* that in spite of that dysfunction, God had a plan and that God's plan was good. If we keep reading Genesis 45, we see that this trust motivated him not to seek revenge, but rather reunion, reconciliation, and redemption.

Review Genesis 45:13. Who did Joseph want a reunion with?

Joseph was not proposing the kind of short-term family reunion where Aunt Sally brings her famous deviled eggs. He wanted to be reunited with his family so they could live together in Egypt.

What does Genesis 45:14–15 expose about Joseph's heart toward his brothers?

The tenderness in these verses reveals that Joseph desired reconciliation. He wanted unity and intimacy, not just proximity.

Is there anyone in your family you long to be reconciled to? If so, is your heart soft toward them? Do you pray for God to bring reconciliation? Take time to write out your prayer now.

Finally, Joseph sought a redemption of all that had been taken from his family. I can hardly wait to show you this!

Read Genesis 45:21–22 and make a list of everything Joseph gave his brothers. Be specific.

They took; he gave. They stripped him of his coat of many colors, shredded it, and dipped it in goat's blood as a cover-up. What did Joseph give each brother in return? "A change of clothes."

How much did Joseph's brothers sell him for? (Refresh your memory with Genesis 37:28.)

What did Joseph give his youngest brother according to verse 22?

Joseph's generosity was more than ten times his brothers' sin. Everything that was taken from him, he returned in increased measure. *This* is redemption: no tally marks, no wound for wound, no forgiveness withheld until it is earned. To be like Joseph—or to be like Jesus—is to extend to our families extravagant generosity and grace, which we cannot drum up on our own. This kind of family is a byproduct of Christ in us.

Do you need God to do one of the Three Rs in your family?

A *Reunion.* Is there someone you love who you are separated from or who has gone ahead of you to heaven? Write their names.

A *Reconciliation.* Is there a fight that has resulted in both sides taking up positions in their corner of the ring? A marriage that has ended? Or a child who has cut off all contact? Write down their names and ask God to bring restoration.

Redemption. Reunions and reconciliations are beautiful things to long for, and God's Word gives us much reason to hope, but what our families really need is redemption, for God to take what is broken and make it whole.

Wrap up today's study by meditating on Colossians 1:10–14.

Let these verses sear your heart with the reminder that redemption is possible because of Jesus. One of the things His sacrifice on the cross teaches us is that there is nothing—*nothing*—He can't redeem. Thank You, Lord!

WEEK 6 | DAY 5

LEAVE A LEGACY OF PRAYER

You can have a profound influence on your family by developing the discipline of prayer. **Take time today to intercede for your family. Use the prompts below as a guide.**

Write down the names of the family members you want to pray for today. Next to each name, write down one need you want to see God meet.

Are there patterns of sin and brokenness that you need God to interrupt? Make a list and pray through it.

What can you praise God for about your family today?

What generational work do you want to see God do in your family? Write it out as a prayer.

Write out Colossians 1:9–11 as a prayer of blessing for your family.

I Am a String in the Bow of the Lord

what:

God allows suffering and struggle for His glory.

so what?

Submit to His stretching for as long as it lasts.

On a recent road trip with my sons, we traveled through the subterranean tunnel beneath Chesapeake Bay. They were all smiles and enthusiasm when we entered the tunnel, but about halfway through, when he could no longer see the light streaming in from either end, my middle son, Judah, said, "This is kinda scary."

WEEK 7

Sometimes in life we can't see the destination God has for us. We don't know when the darkness will lift and the light will come streaming through. Family life is one of the things God has most used to teach me that hoping the path of suffering will be short is a false hope. There is another lesson the story of Joseph teaches: **You are a string in the bow of the Lord.**

In this week's study, you will attend Jacob's funeral and see how Joseph's life profoundly displays the gospel. You'll also wrestle with your "how longs," and see God's target for your family with fresh, gospel clarity.

It's time to **open your Bible** to Genesis 46.

WEEK 7 | DAY 1

SEVENTY SOULS

Big Idea: *God can do a lot with one faithful person.*

READ GENESIS 46:1–27

After nearly two decades of deep grief, Jacob learned that the son he'd been longing for was alive. You can picture the tears welling in his eyes and the wrinkles smoothing in his brow as he whispered, "It is enough; Joseph my son is still alive. I will go and see him before I die" (Gen. 45:28).

Try to put yourself in Jacob's sandals. Wouldn't you start running in the direction of Egypt right away, desperate to hold your long lost son in your arms? But that's not what Jacob did.

What was his first response to this miraculous news according to Genesis 46:1?

This was Jacob's first reaction because he'd built a habit of worshiping the Lord in this way.

Write out the passages listed below. What differences do you see? What similarities?

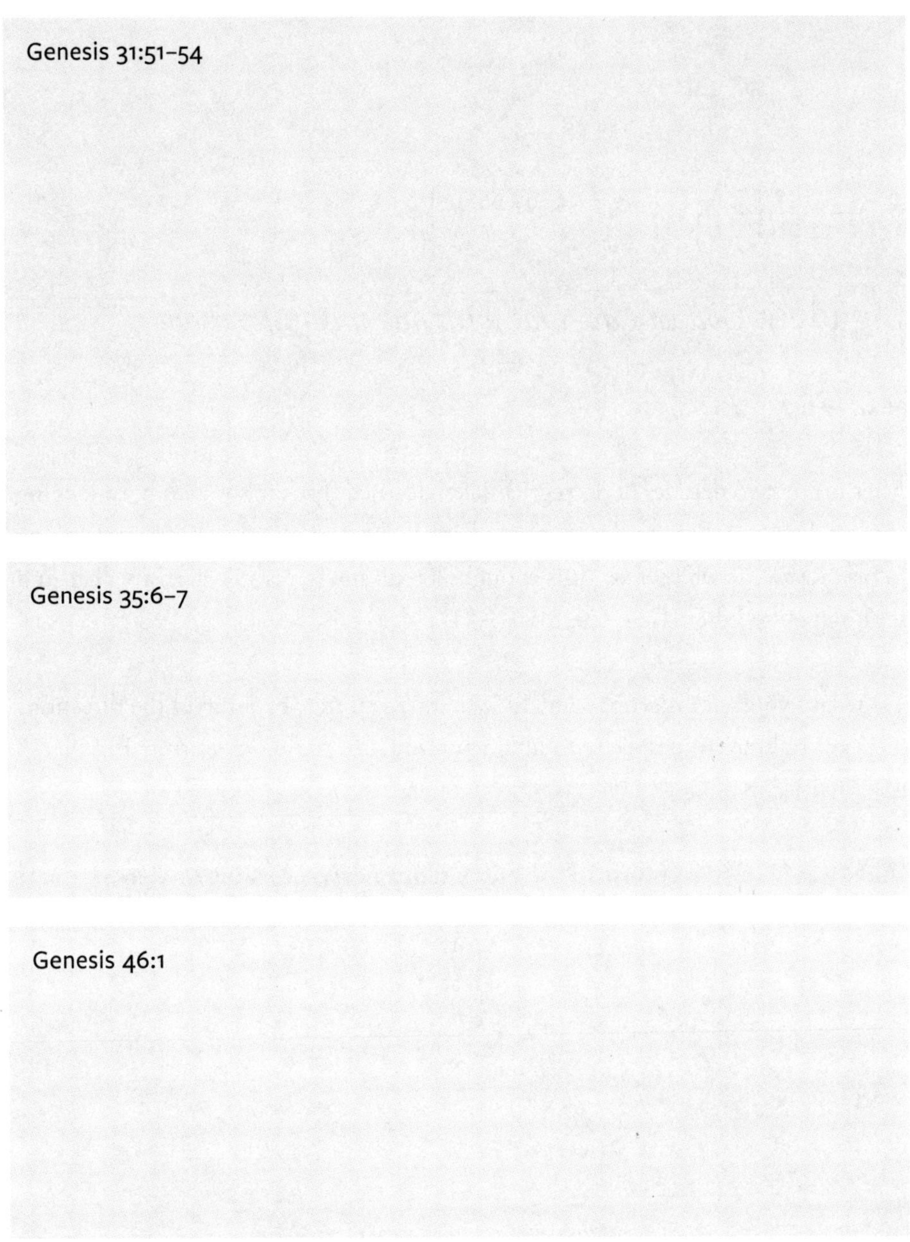

Genesis 31:51–54

Genesis 35:6–7

Genesis 46:1

Jacob learned habits of worship from his grandfather and father. Abraham and Isaac obeyed the Lord in making sacrifices for sin (Gen. 22) and both built altars to the Lord (Gen. 12, 13, 22, 26). Again, we see the baton of faith passed from one generation to the next.

According to Genesis 46:2, how did God speak to Jacob at this time?

What did God say?

What specific promises did God make?

Let's linger here. This was no small ask. Jacob was 130 years old at this point in the story (Gen. 47:9). He wasn't an impetuous man on the run anymore. He'd settled in the land God promised to his grandfather along with his sons, and their sons, and their sons. Surely, we've learned by now that God is less concerned with our comfort than He is with His glory. Obedience to His plan is almost always costly, yet His precious promises are enough.

The promise to make a great nation from this special family is unique. We can't all be patriarchs, but we can have confidence in God's presence.

Write out the verses listed below. What does each one guarantee?

Psalm 145:18

Matthew 28:20

John 14:16–17

Though he couldn't know how every detail of his family's journey would turn out, Jacob did know that God had promised him a lasting legacy, confirmed with His presence. He also had the extra sweet assurance that "Joseph's hand will close your eyes" (Gen. 46:4).

What do you think God meant by that?

How did Jacob respond to God's call according to verses 5–7?

As you think about what you've learned about his life, do you see Jacob's immediate obedience as evidence of heart change? Explain.

The Bible dedicates a couple of short paragraphs to the details of Jacob's call to Egypt, not much when you consider the significance this move will have on the nation of Israel in the rest of Scripture. In contrast, a great deal of ink is spilled listing the genealogy of all those who entered Egypt with Jacob. Again, we see that family matters to God. I hope you've developed your study muscles enough to avoid racing through Scripture's genealogies. The Holy Spirit has preserved them in the canon to teach us something about God.

Read Genesis 46:8–25 in your Bible. As you do:

1. Circle the names of Jacob's sons.
2. Underline Jacob's grandsons.
3. Draw a heart by the names of any women listed.

According to verse 26, how many family members moved to Egypt with Jacob (not counting daughters-in-law)?

Add Joseph's family to the mix, and how big was Jacob's family when he settled in Egypt? (v. 27)

These are not throwaway verses (there are no throwaway verses). Consider what God is showing us. He can take one man—even a rascally one like Jacob—and multiply him into a family of seventy! We can't credit Jacob for this. He made immature and selfish choices again and again, yet the promise of 2 Timothy 2:13 remains: "If we are faithless, he remains faithful." God can do more through the life of one individual, one family, than our hearts have the capacity to hope for.

Consider this:

- A couple has two children who each have two children. By the tenth generation, that couple will be the foreparents of *1,024 descendants.*
- A couple has four children who each have four children. By the tenth generation, that couple will be the foreparents of *1,048,448 descendants.*

Jacob was the father of so many that he got to see the multiplicity of his family within his own lifetime. Only in God's economy can one deceitful man, plus a dysfunctional combination of wives and concubines, equal a flourishing family of seventy. Each person listed in the Genesis 46 genealogy is made in the image of God, deeply loved by God, and able to be used by God to accomplish His purposes on the earth. If God can do that with a family like Joseph's, imagine what He can do with yours as you seek to love and live like Christ!

To wrap up today's study, follow Jacob's lead and worship God. Thank Him for all He has done and all He will do through your family.

WEEK 7 | DAY 2

MORE IN STORE

Big Idea: *God has more blessings in store for you and your family.*

READ GENESIS 46:28–34; 47

One thing the story of Joseph stirs in our hearts is deep gratitude. Through the lens of Joseph's life, we can see that God has done much for our families, despite our failures and fractures. Still, the purpose of the stories of the patriarchs is not just to help us look behind at what God has done. They lift our hearts and minds above and help us rightly long for all God still has in store.

Genesis 46 wraps with a moment of sweet tension that has been building for years. **What can you infer from Joseph's and Jacob's characters from this interaction?**

Joseph was a man who...	Jacob was a man who...

Jacob had his son back. In his mind, that was all he needed. He temporarily forgot about the practical responsibilities of caring for a transplanted family of seventy. Fortunately, Joseph was a man of wisdom and influence. He went to Pharaoh and advocated for his family, another sign that Joseph rejected the bitterness that could have easily taken hold of his heart.

What did Pharaoh promise Joseph in Gen. 47:5–6?

We can't dismiss this as mere human kindness. We know too much! A famine had gripped the land for years and shepherds were seen as the lowest rung of humanity (especially foreign shepherds). Yet, Pharaoh didn't just grant Jacob and his sons land, he put them in charge of his personal livestock, and again God's favor trumps man's plans.

Remind yourself of the truth of Job 42:2. How do you see this at play in Joseph's family?

Perhaps after receiving Pharoah's elaborate provisions, Joseph said something like, "Want to meet my dad?" There's something in each of us that wants to show off the family we love.

Verse 7 tells us, "Joseph brought in Jacob his father and stood him before Pharaoh." What did Jacob do next?

The one who stole the blessings of his brother is now bestowing blessings on the most powerful man in the land. Ah, this is what God can do!

Though Pharaoh granted permission, Joseph was the conduit of blessing to his family.

Review Genesis 47:8–12. List what Joseph did for his father and brothers.

Keep reading through verse 13. What made these blessings extra generous?

This is one more example of Joseph living a righteous life. What principle does 1 Timothy 5:8 teach us?

Why is taking care of our families an outflow of trusting God?

While Joseph did faithfully care for his own, he didn't adopt a circle-the-wagons mentality and serve only those who shared his DNA. The rest of Genesis 47 outlines the ways Joseph managed the citizens of Egypt as the famine worsened. There are details in this chapter that are critical to our understanding of the rest of Genesis and Exodus. We won't follow that trail here, but keep reminding yourself that every text is part of a context. God is always telling a bigger story than what we read on a single page.

Zero in on verses Genesis 47:27–28. How long did Jacob get to live with his sons in Egypt?

What did Jacob say in Genesis 45:28 and Genesis 46:30? Write down his words. Do you think he expected to get to see his family thrive and grow for an additional seventeen years?

How old was Joseph when he was taken from his father according to Genesis 37:2?

God is in the details! He graciously gave Jacob the same number of years with Joseph that he'd had before the pit.

Though he had already richly blessed Jacob many times over, God had more goodness in store. Though He has already blessed your family many times over, He has more in store for you too. Do you believe that, *really believe that?* If you did, could you enjoy your children more? Could you worry less? Could you be more generous toward the faces around your dining room table? I believe the answer is yes.

Consider Ephesians 3:20. What does this verse reveal about what God can do?

The Amplified Bible (AMP) translation phrases this verse as "superabundantly more."[22] Think about how you want to see God bless your family. He can do superabundantly more! Consider the patterns you want Him to break and the wounds you want Him to heal. He can do superabundantly more! Imagine how you want Him to use your family to share His love with others. He can do superabundantly more! God can do more—superabundantly more—for and with and through your family than your wildest hopes and dreams.

As I pen these words, it's "back to school" time for my family. On the first day of the new year, I tiptoed into the living room while it was still quiet and meditated on Ephesians 3:20. I am a part of an accountabiity group of women. We text each other every morning what we've read in the Word. That morning I wrote, "I have faced every other school year with fear. This year, I'm trusting God will keep His Word to do more in the lives of my boys than I can imagine."

How freeing!

We've seen this in the story of Joseph over and over again; but remember, the purpose of preserving Joseph's story in Scripture is not that we'd become enamored with Joseph, but with Jesus. That's why we can't stop reading at Ephesians 3:20.

REMEMBER,
THE PURPOSE OF PRESERVING
JOSEPH'S STORY IN SCRIPTURE
IS NOT THAT WE'D BECOME
ENAMORED WITH JOSEPH,
BUT WITH JESUS.

Write out Ephesians 3:20–21 in the space below.

Though Jacob was content to die at the sight of his son, God had more in store. Though Joseph made wise decisions in Egypt to preserve a single generation, God had more in store. Though God has already blessed and used your family, He has more in store. The goal is His glory, through all generations. Forever and ever. Amen.

WEEK 7 | DAY 3

JACOB'S BLESSINGS

Big Idea: *The words you speak to your family can bring life or death.*

READ GENESIS 48–50

It's easy to think of the people on the pages of our Bibles as caricatures. We picture them in 2D wearing strange robes in desert lands, but they were people made of cells just like us. Keep their humanity in mind as we explore the final days of Jacob.

Though Jacob's death didn't come when he expected, it did come.

Genesis 47 draws to a close with Jacob asking Joseph to swear an oath. What was Jacob's request recorded in verse 29?

Why do you think this was so important to Jacob?

Having secured the promise of a proper burial from his son, Jacob shifted to blessing others. Picture him on his deathbed. He's old and tired. The memories of his life play before him in soft patina. Joseph brings his sons, Manasseh and Ephraim, to visit their dying grandfather.

According to Genesis 48:2, how did Jacob respond to the news that his son was near?

Again, can't you picture him? Sitting up requires all of his strength. Perhaps his breathing is labored. His eyes are weak.

Review Genesis 48:3–7. As he lay there dying, who and what did Jacob want to talk about? Make a list.

Review Genesis 48:8–12. What evidence of tenderness do you see in these verses?

Joseph held his two little boys on his knees, close enough for his dad to see them. Though his eyes were fading, Joseph looked at the faces of Manasseh and Ephraim and saw a future for his family. Like any loving grandparent, he kissed them and hugged them. He loved them. And they loved him.

And though many years had passed, Jacob remembered the lessons he'd learned from his dad, Isaac. Part of being a godly father is blessing the next generation.

Write down Jacob's words from Genesis 48:9–10.

We tend to think of blessing as simply doing something nice for someone, but in the ancient Middle Eastern culture of Joseph, a blessing meant infinitely more. Blessings were not conversations centered on human goodwill, but rather a means of expressing the unique gifts that come from a relationship with God. They were a prayer said out loud asking for God's continued favor and presence.

Jacob gave specific blessings to Joseph, Manasseh, and Ephraim.

Write down the blessing under each name in the chart below.

Joseph	Manasseh	Ephraim

In verse 21, who did Jacob remind Joseph to put his confidence in?

Though Joseph received extra love and attention, he was not an only child. As his strength drained, Jacob called all of his sons together and offered parting words. Some sons received blessings and words of commendation, others were cursed and chastised.

Read Jacob's words from Genesis 49:2–27. Record who received words of praise and who received words of correction in the two columns below.

Praise	Correction

How does Genesis 49:28 describe the words Jacob expressed toward his sons?

Though some of it was surely hard to hear, all of Jacob's words were a blessing because they pointed his sons to who they were and who God had called them to be.

Match the following Proverbs with what each one teaches about life-giving speech.

Proverbs 10:31	"A gentle tongue is a tree of life, but perverseness in it breaks the spirit."
Proverbs 15:4	"There is one whose rash words are like sword thrusts, but the tongue of the wise brings healing."
Proverbs 12:14	"The mouth of the righteous brings forth wisdom, but the perverse tongue will be cut off."
Proverbs 12:18	"From the fruit of his mouth a man is satisfied with good, and the work of a man's hand comes back to him."

Scripture calls each of us to use our words to bring life. That doesn't mean we sugarcoat everything or only say what others want to hear. To be a life-giver is to be a truth-speaker.

Read Proverbs 18:21, which offers a stern warning that applies to every family.

What does this verse teach?

How many families have been torn apart through careless words? How many children bear the scars of their parents' death-giving speech? In contrast, how many beautiful traditions have been passed down through the words expressed within our families? How many hurts have been healed by the encouragement of a family member? How many sinful patterns have been exposed by the loving correction of a parent or grandparent?

You don't have to wait for your deathbed, you know? You can decide to use your words to bless your family today.

What shifts do you need to make to bring more life-giving speech into your home?

WEEK 7 | DAY 4

HOW LONG, O LORD?

Big Idea: *The words you speak to your family can bring life or death.*

GENESIS 50:1–18

"This won't end well, and it won't take long."

That's what the doctor whispered after he told us that my mom had early onset Alzheimer's. In the storm of grief and fear that followed, I grabbed onto those words and held on for dear life. I knew we were heading into a dark tunnel; but I was sure it would be a short tunnel, and I put my hope in that.

Now, several years in, the journey is not ending well, humanly speaking. My mom, the gifted watercolor artist, devoted Gigi, and woman of deep faith in Jesus is fading from one life to the next slowly, *painfully slowly.* And I am learning a good, hard lesson. It's a lesson every follower of Jesus must learn, one our families frequently teach us. It's a lesson I see displayed so profoundly in the life of Joseph: **I am a string in the bow of the Lord.**

Genesis 50 finds Joseph at his father's funeral. How did Joseph respond to his father's death according to verse 1?

Though his dad was imperfect, Joseph loved him deeply. Though his grief was deep, Joseph had a funeral to plan. Verses 2–3 describe a process similar to what you've experienced at the loss of a family member. Joseph also remembered he had a promise to keep.

What loving act did Joseph do for his father as described in verses 4–13?

According to verse 14, who went with Joseph to bury Jacob?

Review Genesis 50:15–18. Funerals have a way of bringing up old junk. What fears and memories came to the surface in the hearts of Joseph's brothers?

In many ways, this whole study has been moving us toward the next few verses. They're stunningly beautiful.

> But Joseph said to them, "Do not fear, for am I in the place of God? As for you, you meant evil against me, but God meant it for good, to bring it about that many people should be kept alive, as they are today." (Gen. 50:19–20)

Now write down Joseph's words recorded in verses 19–20 below.

Who does Joseph focus on in these verses?

We've read Joseph's story in a few chapters of the Bible. Though we don't know every detail, we can see his life from beginning to end. Our lives don't unfold that way. Sometimes reconciliation doesn't come in a few years, or at all. Sometimes the people who threw us in a pit aren't sorry. Sometimes sons aren't reunited with their fathers. Often, our families are the reason we ask a very honest question of God: *How long, O Lord?*

- How long until I receive the family I've been praying for?
- How long until God gives relief?
- How long until my heart is healed?
- How long until our relationship is restored?

- How long until this sickness is cured?
- How long until my prodigal returns?

Take just a moment and ask the Lord: *What's my "how long"?* Write down anything that comes to mind.

Keep Joseph's words to his brothers in mind and turn in your Bible to Psalm 13. Meditate on the words of King David. Underline the phrase "how long" as you read.

How many times did Joseph wonder "how long?" How many times have you? To find hope for our "how longs," we need to keep reading.

If you know David's writing style, you know there's always a pivot point where he shifts his eyes away from his circumstances and trains himself to look toward the character of God.

Write down his words from Psalm 13:5–6 below.

As I've walked the long journey of Alzheimer's and ached to see God move in other areas of my family, I've internalized the truth of Psalm 13 as this prayer: *I am a string in the bow of the Lord.*

God doesn't answer our "how long?" question with answers about time. I've never known anyone who knew exactly how many more days, weeks, months, or years they had to wait for God to move. But through His Word and by His character, we know it's just enough to hit the target He intends.

Joseph experienced this:

- His brothers hated him . . . *stretch.*
- He was sold into slavery . . . *stretch.*
- He was thrown in prison . . . *stretch.*
- Famine came . . . *stretch.*
- His father died . . . *stretch.*

And all along the way, God relieved the tension and then pulled Joseph taught again.

Why? Revisit Joseph's words from Genesis 50:20.

We could sum it up this way: So God would get the glory.

You are a string in the bow of the Lord. He will pull you back exactly as long as He needs to, not one second longer, to hit the target—*His target.* The bull's-eye our families are meant to hit is *His glory.*

To wrap up this session, read through Psalm 13 below again. After each stanza, I've left a space for you to write: "I am a string in the bow of the Lord."

How long, O LORD? Will you forget me forever?
How long will you hide your face from me?

How long must I take counsel in my soul
and have sorrow in my heart all the day?
How long shall my enemy be exalted over me?

Consider and answer me, O LORD my God;
light up my eyes, lest I sleep the sleep of death,

lest my enemy say, "I have prevailed over him,"
lest my foes rejoice because I am shaken.

But I have trusted in your steadfast love;
my heart shall rejoice in your salvation.

I will sing to the LORD,
because he has dealt bountifully with me.

WEEK 7 | DAY 5

LEAVE A LEGACY OF PRAYER

You can have a profound influence on your family by developing the discipline of prayer. **Take time today to intercede for your family. Use the prompts below as a guide.**

Write down the names of the family members you want to pray for today. Next to each name, write down one need you want to see God meet.

Are there patterns of sin and brokenness that you need God to interrupt? Make a list and pray through it.

What can you praise God for about your family today?

What generational work do you want to see God do in your family? Write it out as a prayer.

Write out 2 Thessalonians 3:16 as a prayer of blessing for your family.

Nurseries for Heaven

what:

Our families point us to the hope of heaven.

so what?

Love your family well today as a means of celebrating your hope in tomorrow.

There's a Puritan prayer I love. It goes like this:

> Sanctify and prosper my domestic devotion,
> instruction, discipline, example,
> that my house may be a nursery for heaven,
> my church the garden of the Lord,
> enriched with trees of righteousness of thy planting;
> for thy glory . . . Amen.[23]

WEEK 8

Don't you love the imagery of our homes being nurseries for heaven? Think of our families as incubators where the things of God can grow. Remember that family is God's plan for the flourishing of mankind, and as we've seen from Joseph's life, He doesn't only use perfect families to accomplish this. (Good news since there are no perfect families.)

In this week's study, you'll stand in the shadow of Joseph's sarcophagus. Though they've long disintegrated, his bones still speak a message about the faithfulness of God. You'll also map the trials your family has faced and learn to see them from a different paradigm. As you close the cover of this study, you'll be reminded that loving your family is an act of radical resistance against the darkness.

LOVING YOUR FAMILY IS
AN ACT OF RADICAL RESISTANCE
AGAINST THE DARKNESS.

It's time for me to say my favorite words one last time.

Open your Bible to Genesis 50:22–26.

WEEK 8 | DAY 1

ENDING AT THE BEGINNING

Big idea: *Joseph's last sermon declared the faithfulness of God.*

READ GENESIS 50:22–26

Our deep dive into the story of Joseph started at his funeral. It's fitting that that's where we will also end, but as you'll see in today's study, Joseph's death wasn't an ending at all. As it is for all of us who trust in the God of Abraham, Isaac, and Jacob, death is actually a beautiful beginning.

Review Genesis 50:22–26 below. Underline any family language you find in this passage.

> **22** So Joseph remained in Egypt, he and his father's house. Joseph lived 110
> years. **23** And Joseph saw Ephraim's children of the third generation. The
> children also of Machir the son of Manasseh were counted as Joseph's own. **24**
> And Joseph said to his brothers, "I am about to die, but God will visit you and
> bring you up out of this land to the land that he swore to Abraham, to Isaac,
> and to Jacob." **25** Then Joseph made the sons of Israel swear, saying, "God will
> surely visit you, and you shall carry up my bones from here." **26** So Joseph died,
> being 110 years old. They embalmed him, and he was put in a coffin in Egypt.

What did Joseph make his brothers promise? (v. 25)

Why do you think he asked this of them?

Joseph's request doesn't reveal some strange superstition that he believed that the location of his bones mattered after death. He hadn't adopted the pagan beliefs of his Egyptian neighbors regarding the afterlife. This request was, in many ways, the final sermon of Joseph's life.

Remember, who was Joseph's great-grandfather?

What did God promise Abraham in Genesis 12:1–3?

God kept His promise. *God always keeps His promise.* He did show Abraham the land of Canaan. It was the place where Isaac married Rebekah and they had twin boys: Esau and Jacob. Joseph knew what it was like to live in the land of God's promise. That's where he grew up, and even though he'd seen his dad take his last breath in Egypt, just as he was about to do, Joseph's faith in God did not waver. He knew:

- No human hatred could separate him from God.
- No pit could prevent God from keeping His promises.
- No famine could cut him off from God's blessing.

In every season of his life, even as he lay on his deathbed in foreign territory, Joseph saw that he was safe and secure in the palm of God's hand.

Read Romans 8:35–36. Though these words were written by Paul, millennia after the days of Joseph, they aptly describe what Joseph went through. Which of the trials that Paul mentioned did Joseph face? Make a list.

Joseph's life also illustrates the rest of Paul's thinking recorded in Romans 8.

Write out Romans 8:37–39. Savor these words as you write them.

Did any of his trials separate Joseph from God's love? How do you know?

Joseph trusted the love and faithfulness of God through the many highs and lows of his life. He also trusted that God was going to keep the promise He made to bring nations and kings from his family, despite their deep dysfunction.

Hebrews 11:22 lists two things as evidence of Joseph's faith. What were they?

Joseph didn't need his bones where he was going. Remember how wise he was? He surely knew that! But he did need the God of his forefathers. Even with his final breaths, he proclaimed that his faith was in Yahweh.

As we read the final verses of Genesis and turn the page to Exodus, we see Joseph's name again.

What does Exodus 1:8 record?

While God is always doing a generational work, so is Satan. A new pharaoh would soon come into power, one who would enslave the descendants of Joseph. Hard times were ahead for this family, but just like He did for Joseph, God would redeem it.

If I were writing Joseph's story, I'd put Exodus 13:19 on the final page.

Who carried Joseph's bones back to Canaan?

Finally, after so much turmoil, *Joseph got to go home.*

I think we love the story of Joseph so much because we can all identify with it.

- We know what it's like to have families fractured by sin.
- We know what it's like to be betrayed by the ones who share our last name.
- We know what it's like to be pulled from one pit only to be thrown into another.
- We know what it's like to be separated from the ones we love.
- We know what it's like to long for the redemption of all that is broken and fractured in our families and in our world.

We also know what it's like to have a God who keeps His promise that He has so much more in store. The application here is as obvious as it is beautiful.

Revelation 21:1–4 are my favorite verses in the entire Scriptures. I turn to them so often, the page has been pulled from the binding of my Bible. I have to tuck it back in every time I open the Word.

What do these verses promise?

The promised land of Joseph's day was made of dirt, much like your home is built on. It was a gift, to be sure, but it could only ever be temporary as "the world is passing away along with its desires" (1 John 2:17). For those of us in Christ, a new and better land is promised, a place where grief and sadness and suffering have been banished to the pit and we get to dwell with God forever.

Your family may remain fractured in this life . . .

Your prodigal children may not return to God in your time frame . . .

Patterns of sin that have gripped your family may continue to wreak havoc for a while . . .

But because God is faithful, soon enough, *you'll get to go home* to be a part of the family of God forever. Joseph's story didn't end in death. Because of Jesus, your story—and your family's story—won't either.

To wrap up today's study, write out a prayer thanking God for the promise of heaven. Ask Him to help you trust His promises all the way to the end.

WEEK 8 | DAY 2

JESUS IS THE BETTER JOSEPH

Big idea: *The story of Joseph is ultimately about the gospel.*

READ GENESIS 50:19–21; HEBREWS 9:27–28

As we drop the landing gear on this study and begin our descent, I hope you're thinking about Joseph less and less and thinking about Jesus more and more. I can't remind you too often that the point of reading our Bibles is not to memorize facts or to learn more about ourselves. The reason we study is to learn more about God. When we understand His character, we are better able to reflect His image and share His light to a dark and hurting world.

Think back to Week 4, Day 2 where we learned that Jesus is the "Rosetta Stone" that helps us rightly understand and apply all of Scripture. How has knowing the character of Jesus helped you understand the story of Joseph? Make a list.

Read both passages listed on each line below. Write what is similar between Jesus and Joseph in the blank.

Genesis 37:4 ________________________________ Isaiah 53:3

Genesis 37:36 ________________________________ Matthew 2:13–15

Genesis 37:28 ________________________________ Matthew 26:14–15

Genesis 39:20 ________________________________ John 18:12

Genesis 43:30 ________________________________ Matthew 9:36

This is just a sampling of the parallels we can make; and while that exercise is fascinating, it can also cause us to miss the forest for the trees. The most important connection point between Joseph and Jesus—the one we simply can't miss if we are going to grasp the beauty and meaning of this story—is the gospel.

Now's a good time for me to ask: What is the gospel? Write your answer below.

It's my experience that women who have been truly transformed by Jesus, who love their Bibles, and are serious about making disciples, can still struggle to articulate the gospel. Part of that is because it is a supernatural work of God our finite brains can struggle to wrap themselves around, but we also tend to overcomplicate it. Let's break it down.

According to Romans 3:23, who has sinned?

Because God is holy, He cannot tolerate our sin. What consequence does all sin have in our relationship with God according to Isaiah 59:2?

That separation takes the form of death according to Romans 6:23. What beautiful promise does the rest of that verse promise?

You are a sinner. You've *always* been a sinner (Ps. 51:5). It's worse than that. As we've faced many times over the course of this study, your entire family is made up of sinners, separated from God and headed toward eternal punishment. You cannot save yourself from sin and its consequences, and you cannot save the ones you love. That's the cloud, and what a dark and terrifying cloud it is. But there is a silver lining.

What hope does Romans 5:6–11 give?

This is the gospel! We were dead and buried beneath the weight of our rebellion against God, but Jesus went to the cross, paid the price required for our sin, making a way for us and our families to experience eternal celebration with Him.

With the gospel fresh in our minds, let's revisit the keystone verse of Joseph's story: Genesis 50:20. Write out the passages listed in the chart below. Draw arrows to connect any parallels you see.

Genesis 50:20	Hebrews 9:27–28

God sent Joseph ahead to Egypt to save many from starvation, a miracle, for sure, but it's nothing compared to what He did through Jesus. The Father sent Jesus to the cross to save many from their sins. How many exactly? Only heaven will tell, but if you've surrendered your life to Jesus, you've been saved from the punishment you deserve. You've been moved from death to life (John 5:24)!

How does Psalm 40:2 describe this lavish gift of grace?

Like Joseph, and only because of Jesus, you've been pulled from the pit. **Joseph's story is a gospel story**. Satan intends harm against God's children. He hates us. He hates our families. But God can take what the enemy means for evil and turn it for good. Jesus is our proof.

Would you wrap up today's study by singing "Amazing Grace"? Remind yourself that Jesus' sacrifice pulled you from the pit, and that Satan's evil plan for your destruction has been permanently thwarted by God's elaborate grace.

WEEK 8 | DAY 3

THE CURVEBALLS KEEP COMING

Big Idea: *Your family's greatest trials are opportunities to experience God's love.*

READ HEBREWS 11; PSALM 34:19; ACTS 14:21–22

We look at the brokenness in our families and we want a solution, preferably a quick one. Perhaps you picked up this study hoping to find a way to communicate with your daughter-in-law, or reason with your unbelieving husband, or get past the wounds inflicted by your parents.

God is not immune to your practical needs. Through His Word He invites you to cast it all on Him because He cares about you deeply (1 Peter 5:7). He also knows that human solutions can only ever be temporary. While His Word helps us, it is not primarily a self-help tool. It is meant to get our eyes off our struggles and onto the One who is at work to redeem them.

A painful reality we see illustrated in the lives of many Bible characters, including Joseph, is that God allows suffering in the lives of those He dearly loves.

Joseph's name is listed among some of the most faithful examples of our faith in Hebrews 11, a chapter often referred to as The Great Hall of Faith.

Skim those verses in Hebrews 11 again. Make a list of the trials God's elect were forced to endure.

Though many elements of Joseph's story were redeemed in his lifetime, others weren't, and Joseph's death did not mark the end of his family's struggle. Jesus doesn't intend to trick us into thinking that we can move our families toward a place of complete unity and ease. He said, "This world will keep throwing you curveballs" (John 16:33, Erin Davis translation). Yet, your family will never face any hardship without the promise of God's love, presence, and plan.

Take some time to draw a timeline of your family's greatest hardships. The next two pages are dedicated to this activity. Use the vertical line on the left side to plot seasons of suffering, sickness, or sorrow. Write down details next to each data point.

Read Acts 14:21–22. What do these verses say we must go through to enter the kingdom of God?

What do you think that means?

Suffering isn't the entry fee to heaven. Jesus took care of that. But as fallen sinners in a fallen world, suffering is inevitable. God's Word combined with our human experience shows us that the path between here and glory is fraught with land mines. Sure, the promise of heaven is enough to carry us through, but God has also provided blessed hope in the midst of the struggle.

Look up the following verses. Write down what each one promises.

Deuteronomy 31:8

Isaiah 41:13

Isaiah 43:2

Psalm 34:18

Romans 8:28

God may not take all of your family's suffering away in your timing, just as He didn't with Joseph, but He will never leave you. He will help you. He will use the hard things for your good and His glory.

Revisit the timeline you drew on pages 241 and 242. Notice the blank line on the right side of the pages. On this line, mark the points in your life when you've experienced the greatest intimacy with Jesus. As you look at the two lines, what conclusions can you draw about the ways trials draw your heart toward the Lord?

As for Joseph, God was with him in the pit. God was with him in prison. God was with him during years of abundance. God was with him during years of famine. When he had no one else to turn to, God was there. When he was the man of the hour everyone depended on to save them, God was there too.

What if the struggles your family faces are the microphone you need to magnify the voice of God? What if these temporary trials are His way of teaching you that He can be fully trusted?

To wrap up today's study, doodle around Psalm 34:17–19 below. Thank the Lord for His presence and His promise of future deliverance.

17 When the righteous cry for help, the LORD hears
and delivers them out of all their troubles.

18 The LORD is near to the brokenhearted
and saves the crushed in spirit.

19 Many are the afflictions of the righteous,
but the LORD delivers him out of them all.

WEEK 8 | DAY 4

BEDROCK HOUSES

Big Idea: *Build your family on the solid rock of God's Word.*

READ MATTHEW 7:24–27

Wow, sister. We've journeyed a long way. I've loved every second of our time together, but life is calling. Our marriages need tending to. Our children need to be cared for. Our parents need a phone call. Our siblings need an invitation to dinner. I hope all this talk about family has helped you see the people on your family tree with fresh love and grace.

We've spent eight sessions asking, "What does the Bible say about our families?" Let's ask another layer of that same question: What does Jesus say? As is so often the case when we open our Bibles, we find that He doesn't give us a straightforward to-do list. Instead, He offers a dichotomy.

Review Matthew 7:24–27.

What will happen to the house built on the rock when trials come?

What will happen to the house built on the sand when trials come?

What is the big idea of what Jesus was teaching here?

The same concept is given in a verse you examined earlier in this study. What does Psalm 127:1 teach?

These passages aren't giving advice for the construction of physical houses, but rather what we build our families on—what we build our lives on.

Look up the following verses. What (or who) does each one identify as the rock?

Psalm 18:2

Psalm 62:7

Psalm 89:26

Psalm 95:1

Psalm 144:1

We can build our families on the Word of God, which reveals the character of God, which can never be separated from the redemptive plan of God. "The rock" is not some abstract idea. The rock is a person; His name is Jesus.

Jesus said something else about family. I'll admit, it can be a harder pill to swallow at first.

Write down Jesus' words from Luke 14:26.

What do you think He meant?

This is a good example of why we need good hermeneutics. We let Scripture interpret Scripture. Was Jesus contradicting the Ten Commandments that call us to honor our father and mother? The context of Luke 14 shows us that those who were listening to Jesus teach were making excuses about why they couldn't follow them. Many pointed to their families.

We do that too:

- I can't take time to sit in Your Word. I have children to take care of.
- I can't submit to my husband. He's a weak leader.
- I can't go to church. I can't get the little ones ready.
- I can't forgive my parents. They've hurt me too much.

Jesus is calling us to love Him so much that our devotion to our human families pales in comparison, so much so that it looks like a polar opposite emotion.

Our human families are not our ultimate family. They're meant to tell the story that we were once orphans, fatherless, and separated from our spiritual siblings; but Jesus went to the cross to make a way for us to be reconciled to the Father and adopted into the family of God.

Through this study, you've learned some important lessons about God's design for the family.

Repeat the truths below by writing them as "I believe" statements. (Example: "I believe that family is God's idea.")

Family is God's good plan for the flourishing of mankind.

God is doing a generational work in your family.

The enemy seeks to do generational damage to your family.

God is able to work the challenges and heartaches your family faces to your good for His glory.

There is brokenness in every family.

God can do a redemptive work in every family.

You are part of God's family forever.

Family is God's idea and God can work—God is working—even in the most dysfunctional parts of your family. We can apply all we've seen in the story of Joseph by letting this shift the way we reach toward and respond to those we love.

WEEK 8 | DAY 5

LEAVE A LEGACY OF PRAYER

You can have a profound influence on your family by developing the discipline of prayer. **Take time today to intercede for your family. Use the prompts below as a guide.**

Write down the names of the family members you want to pray for today. Next to each name, write down one need you want to see God meet.

Are there patterns of sin and brokenness that you need God to interrupt? Make a list and pray through it.

What can you praise God for about your family today?

What generational work do you want to see God do in your family? Write it out as a prayer.

Write out Philippians 2:14–16 as a prayer of blessing for your family.

A FINAL WORD ON YOUR FOREVER FAMILY

The first church Jason and I attended as a married couple had a long-standing tradition for how they closed every service. At the pastor's direction, the entire congregation would join hands across the aisles and sing these words in unison:

> I'm so glad I'm a part of the family of God.
> I've been washed in the fountain,
> Cleansed by His blood.
> Joint heirs with Jesus as we travel this sod.
> I'm a part of the family, the family of God.[22]

Teenagers would smile shyly as they grabbed the hand of the boy or girl they had a crush on; school-aged boys would turn the exercise into an arm wrestling match while mommas shushed nearby; sweet old ladies would often squeeze your hand a few times as you sang. We were imperfect people, imperfectly worshiping a perfect Savior. We've moved away from that community and now attend the church where I came to Christ, but every Sunday (and all the days in between), my heart repeats that refrain. I am *so* glad I'm a part of the family of God. Let's marvel at the heritage we've been promised!

> **14** For all who are led by the Spirit of God are sons [and daughters] of
> God. **15** For you did not receive the spirit of slavery to fall back into fear,
> but you have received the Spirit of adoption as sons, by whom we cry, "Abba!
> Father!" **16** The Spirit himself bears witness with our spirit that we are
> children of God, **17** and if children, then heirs—heirs of God and fellow
> heirs with Christ, provided we suffer with him in order that we may also be
> glorified with him. (Rom. 8:14–17)

Thanksgiving dinners and Saturday morning pancakes. Celebrations and sad goodbyes. Good memories and difficult ones. Shared genetics and opposing views.

These are some of the threads that weave in and out of our families. For each of us, family is as complex as it is beautiful. Joseph's story has reminded me of this truth again and again and provided me with profound hope that God is the One masterfully weaving the story of my family, and yours, for His glory.

But again, that is just the lower story. We are part of a supernatural and eternal family. We have spiritual siblings from every tongue, tribe, and nation and together we will inherit a kingdom—the kingdom of Jesus Christ! *This* is the message of family Scripture declares most loudly. *This* is the truest meaning of the story of Joseph.

God's Word also calls us to endeavor to make life on earth a reflection of the life we will someday experience in heaven (Matt. 6:10). This study has helped me see my family as my first neighbors, the ones to whom I am most often and urgently called to love according to Jesus' command, "love your neighbor as yourself" (Mark 12:31). So, as we close the covers of this book, let's do it with commitment to infuse our families with the love and words of Jesus and with unsinkable hope that the family of our dreams is ours thanks to Jesus.

NOTES

1. Emily Osterloff, "The Wonderfully Weird World of Tenrecs," Natural History Museum, August 23, 2024, https://www.nhm.ac.uk/discover/the-weird-world-of-tenrecs.html.
2. "Seven Animals Who Mate for Life," BBC Earth, August 23, 2024, https://www.bbcearth.com/news/seven-animals-who-mate-for-life.
3. Adapted from the song "Father Abraham Had Many Sons," Pierre Kartner, https://americansongwriter.com/who-wrote-the-traditional-campfire-song-father-abraham/.
4. *The Holy Bible*, English Standard Version (Crossway, 2001), 23.
5. Mike Campbell, "Meaning, Origin and History of the Name Joseph," *Behind the Name*, https://www.behindthename.com/name/joseph.
6. Foy Scalf, "The Rosetta Stone: Unlocking the Ancient Egyptian Language," American Research Center in Egypt, August 22, 2024, https://arce.org/resource/rosetta-stone-unlocking-ancient-egyptian-language/.
7. "Rosetta Stone," BYU Idaho, August 22, 2024, https://spc.byui.edu/exhibits/exhibitions/5-rosettastone.
8. Adapted from Erin Davis, *7 Feasts: Finding Christ in the Sacred Celebrations of the Old Testament* (Moody Publishers, 2020), 17–18, 20.
9. Erik Raymond, "The Wonderful Similarities Between Joseph and Jesus," The Gospel Coalition, March 6, 2018, https://www.thegospelcoalition.org/blogs/erik-raymond/wonderful-similarities-joseph-jesus/.
10. Raymond, "The Wonderful Similarities."
11. John Piper, "God is Always Doing 10,000 Things in Your Life," Desiring God, January 1, 2013, https://www.desiringgod.org/articles/god-is-always-doing-10000-things-in-your-life.
12. Greg Thomas, "Can You Break the Cycle of Generational Dysfunction?," *Good News*, November 27, 2007, https://www.ucg.org/the-good-news/can-you-break-the-cycle-of-generational-dysfunction.
13. "Mandragora Officinarum, Mandrake," UST Medicinal Garden, August 22, 2024, https://ustbiologymedicinalgarden.wordpress.com/mandragora-officinarum-mandrake/.
14. Kate Quarry and Lalita Kaplish, "Mandrake Medicine and Myths," Welcome Collection, March 29, 2022, https://wellcomecollection.org/articles/YjCgGhIAACAA3SSh.
15. "Genesis 25:26," bibleref.com, https://www.bibleref.com/biblepassage/Printer?section=Genesis_25:26&lang=en.
16. *Merriam-Webster.com Dictionary*, s.v. "epigenetics," accessed August 20, 2024, https://www.merriam-webster.com/dictionary/epigenetics.
17. Rachel Zimmerman, "How Does Trauma Spill From One Generation to the Next?", *The Washington Post,* June 12, 2023, https://www.washingtonpost.com/wellness/2023/06/12/generational-trauma-passed-healing/.
18. Ann Gold Buscho, "Are Kids More Likely to Divorce If Their Parents Did?," *Psychology Today*, August 15, 2023, https://www.psychologytoday.com/us/blog/a-better-divorce/202306/are-your-children-more-likely-to-divorce-if-you-divorce.
19. Robert Frost, *The Poetry of Robert Frost* (Henry Holt, 1969), 105.
20. Adapted from Erin Davis, "Hospitality Toward the Indwelling God," Revive Our Hearts, April 30, 2024, https://www.reviveourhearts.com/blog/hospitality-toward-the-indwelling-god/.
21. Robert Frost, "Stopping by Woods on a Snowy Evening," *The Poetry of Robert Frost: The Collected Poems,* ed. Edward Connery Lathem (Holt Paperbacks, 2002), 224.
22. Ephesians 3:20, *The Holy Bible: The Amplified Bible* (The Lockman Foundation, 1987, 2015).
23. Arthur Bennett, ed., *The Valley of Vision* (The Banner of Truth Trust, 1975), 113.